STICKY FAITH

LAUNCH KIT

YOUR NEXT

180
DAYS

TOWARD STICKY FAITH

KARA POWELL

FULLER YOUTH INSTITUTE

FULLER YOUTH INSTITUTE

Sticky Faith Launch Kit
Your Next 180 Days Toward Sticky Faith

Published in the United States of America by
Fuller Youth Institute, 135 N. Oakland Ave., Pasadena, CA, 91182
fulleryouthinstitute.org

ISBN 978-0-615-86144-9

Cover and Interior Design: FiveStone
Copy Editor: Dana Wilkerson

Printed in the United States of America

ACKNOWLEDGMENTS

This Launch Kit is truly a collaborative work representing hours of conversations, brainstorming, hands-on work, and writing. We would like to particularly note the following contributors: Scott Cormode, Jake Mulder, Daniel Sichin Kim, Nate Stratman, Josh Bishop, Meredith Miller, Steve Argue, Matthew DePrez, Steven Johnson, and Jeff Mattesich.

We would also like to thank all of the Sticky Faith Cohort participants from the past four years, without whose hard work and trial and error there would be no Launch Kit! We're grateful to the following friends of FYI who contributed Launch Tips: Jay Clark, April Diaz, Katye Dunn, Lauren Eden, Kris Fernhout, David Fraze, Tim Galleher, Bill Haslim, Keegan Lenker, Alan Mercer, John Rosensteel, and Nate Roskam.

Thanks to Paul Sun for always being "on call" to shoot a video for FYI.

Deep gratitude goes to the rest of our fantastic FYI team for making this possible: Haley Smith, Irene Cho, Matthew Schuler, and Davin Tang. It is a joy to ride the wave of this Sticky Faith Movement with you.

PRAISE FOR STICKY FAITH

One of the many reasons I'm a huge fan of Sticky Faith is because it's so timely! The Sticky Faith content is helping move youth and family ministry in the direction we all need to head. It not only raises crucial questions about the gospel, the church, and families, but it also provides practical answers and ideas any youth leader can try.

DOUG FIELDS
VETERAN YOUTH WORKER AND
YOUTH SPECIALTIES ADVISOR

Kara Powell approaches her work as a sacred calling and with a fierce confidence that God can handle whatever troubling data the research might reveal about young people — and about ourselves.

KENDA CREASY DEAN
PROFESSOR OF YOUTH,
CHURCH AND CULTURE AT
PRINCETON SEMINARY

Sticky Faith will change the way you see the role of your church in building authentic faith in the next generation. This is starting a critical conversation with parents and leaders that should reshape the church.

REGGIE JOINER
FOUNDER OF THE RETHINK
GROUP, LEADER OF THE
ORANGE CONFERENCE

I couldn't be more thrilled with the *Sticky Faith Launch Kit*! For years, I've wanted to have an accessible resource to put in the hands of churches trying to implement a more family-based youth ministry. This kit far exceeds my expectations! I can't wait to make it available to the churches we work with.

MARK DEVRIES
PRESIDENT,
YOUTH MINISTRY ARCHITECTS

A word to those who are joining the Sticky Faith Movement: "Easy to follow" does not mean "Easy to implement." Change in any system is often a treacherous adventure. The uniqueness of this *Launch Kit* is found in the way Kara and Brad practically walk you through the challenges inherent in making your church a Sticky Faith community.

DR. DAVID FRAZE
DIRECTOR OF STUDENT MINISTRIES,
THE HILLS CHURCH OF CHRIST,
Richland, Texas

The *Sticky Faith Launch Kit* is a profoundly practical and deeply robust toolkit for equipping your church to become "sticky." The team at the Fuller Youth Institute have put their research and proven methodology to work here. Theory and research meet the real world in ways that youth workers, church staff, volunteers, and parents will find understandable, accessible, and practical. Do you want to lead change in your church? *The Sticky Faith Launch Kit* is for you.

ALAN MERCER
EXECUTIVE PASTOR, CHRIST
COMMUNITY CHURCH,
Leawood, Kansas

TABLE OF CONTENTS

LAUNCH NOW!

IN YOUR HANDS IS
EVERYTHING YOU NEED
TO BEGIN TO IMPLEMENT
STICKY FAITH IN YOUR
YOUTH MINISTRY AND
ENTIRE CHURCH.

READY TO GET STARTED?
REGISTER ONLINE NOW AT
STICKYFAITHLAUNCHKIT.ORG
TO ACCESS LOADS OF EXTRA
RESOURCES AND JOIN OUR
ONLINE COMMUNITY.

THE REGISTRATION CODE
FOR CREATING A NEW USER
ACCOUNT IS **VDAZ88Q**

MODULE 01

YOU AND YOUR LAUNCH TEAM

Part 1

HOW NOT TO GET STUCK ON THE LAUNCH PAD

One of the iconic images of late twentieth century America was the space shuttle launch countdown. Many of us can remember watching launches on television as kids and staging launches of our own from our couches or back porches.

While we typically think of shuttle launches in "T minus 10 seconds" terms, the T (test) clock actually starts at T-43 hours.

Forty-three hours? You read it right. There are checklists of hundreds of details that must be resolved prior to the final countdown seconds.[1] And, of course, the training leading up to those forty-three hours takes months—years, really.

Despite any grandiose dreaming we might have done as kids, none of us would actually show up at the Kennedy Space Center and attempt to launch a shuttle into orbit.

Why then do we think we can do the same thing in our churches?

Every day at the Fuller Youth Institute we work with youth workers and church leaders from around the country. More intensively, we've been working with 100 churches through our Sticky Faith Cohort process over the past four years to help them implement change in their youth ministries and congregations. We've learned a few things through this journey:

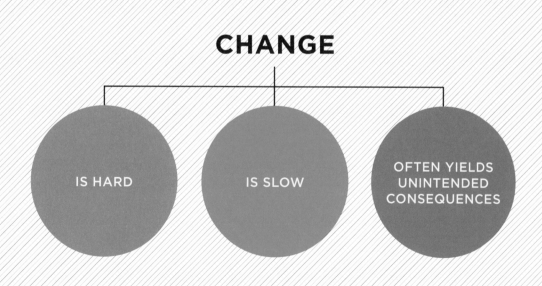

CHANGE

IS HARD

IS SLOW

OFTEN YIELDS UNINTENDED CONSEQUENCES

1   For a quick look, see this list on Wikipedia: http://en.wikipedia.org/wiki/Space_shuttle_launch_countdown.

And along the way, people quit. Good leaders, armed with knowledge and guts, get discouraged and give up. They hit roadblocks they can't seem to work around. They face summits that seem insurmountable. One parent too many sends a discouraging email, or the pastor confronts them about a drop in attendance, and they give up.

But as leaders, if we're going to impact young people in our congregations, sometimes we have to change. More specifically, we have to learn to *lead change*. And that prospect often stops us in our tracks.

In your hands is a different approach to both change and *leading* change. **We're calling it a *Launch Kit* because we believe it will lead you through a strategic implementation process that will transform your church.** We've tested the process with over one hundred churches from across the country. We're not naïve to the challenges in your unique context; every community has challenges. Yet we put this kit together because we believe *you can be a change agent* in your congregation. And you can start today.

CONSIDER THIS DAY 1

In front of you lies a plan to shape the next 179 days of your ministry. It's not just a program, though we will give you some practical tools. More than that, it's a *process* to contextualize and launch Sticky Faith in your church. Imagine this like a **coach in a box,** ready to talk you through the steps you'll need to take in order to get your ministry off the ground and help it fly.

But first we need to gather on the launch pad.

 ▶ **ADDITIONAL RESOURCES**
DON'T WALK ALONE

One of the reasons we hope you will register your Launch Kit right away at stickyfaithlaunchkit.org is to connect you with a broader community of like-minded travelers. When we gather leaders in the same room we find it to be rich soil for innovative thinking. A goal of our online Launch Kit portal is to cultivate a similar context for conversation around the questions you're most interested in exploring. Join us now! See page 1 for details.

IMAGINE THIS LIKE A COACH IN A BOX, READY TO TALK YOU THROUGH THE STEPS YOU'LL NEED TO TAKE IN ORDER TO GET YOUR MINISTRY OFF THE GROUND AND HELP IT FLY.

Part 2

WHAT'S MY ROLE IN BUILDING STICKY FAITH?

Insanity has been defined as doing the same thing over and over, yet expecting different results.[1]

Tragically, this is what many of us do in our ministries day after day and year after year. In order to develop Sticky Faith, the first step is to understand *what* needs to change. The second (and usually more difficult) step is to actually *make* these changes.

In order to help you, your team, and your church take steps toward making changes stick, we've partnered with Fuller Seminary's leadership guru, Dr. Scott Cormode, to create video modules to address questions that frequently pop up as leaders begin to navigate change:

» Why are people afraid of change?
» How can we communicate better about changes we want to make?
» How do I help my senior pastor understand what needs to change?

 ▶ **INSTRUCTIONAL NOTE**
WE'LL CUE YOU HERE IN THE TEXT WHEN IT'S
TIME TO WATCH A VIDEO WITH THIS ICON:

While it might be tempting to just skip the videos and read on, we think your experience will be richer if you take a few moments to watch each short (generally less than five minutes) video and then share them with your core team members. Plus, we get a kick out of telling you what to do, so just humor us along the way.

So let's buckle up together and get ready for the launch journey. Your next step is to watch the *What is Sticky Faith?* video and read on.

 ▶ **VIDEO**
Download the 4-minute "What is Sticky Faith?" video at stickyfaithlaunchkit.org.

---

1   This definition is commonly attributed to Albert Einstein.

Part 3

WHAT IS STICKY FAITH? HOW DO I EXPLAIN IT TO OTHERS?

Before you launch *anything,* we want you to have a solid grasp on what Sticky Faith is and what it means for your ministry.

We often hear of leaders who reduce Sticky Faith to *one* principle, *one* program, or *one* strategy. If it were that easy, we'd have written a "do this one thing" book by now. We'd also be driving nicer cars. But the truth is, Sticky Faith is much more complex than any one approach to discipleship.

▶ ADDITIONAL RESOURCES
READ MORE

See stickyfaith.org/about-sticky-faith/ to read more about our research and resources, particularly detailed in the books *Sticky Faith* and *Sticky Faith: Youth Worker Edition.* The good news is that Zondervan is partnering with us to provide discounts to leaders like you who have purchased the Sticky Faith Launch Kit. Using the code "launchkit" at churchsource.com you can get a 30 percent discount on 1-5 copies, a 40 percent discount on 6-19 copies, and a 50 percent discount (wow!) on 20 or more copies of any *Sticky Faith* resource for your congregation. Plus free shipping on orders over $50. Call 1-800-727-3480 or visit churchsource.com to order.

You may have already read one of our *Sticky Faith* books or heard us speak at a conference, or maybe you've spent time on stickyfaith.org. Following up on your prior encounters with Sticky Faith, this section can serve as both a primer and a reference tool to help you succinctly summarize Sticky Faith for others in your context.

LAUNCH TIP

"Sticky Faith gives legitimacy to what otherwise might be considered just one youth pastor's ideas and perspectives. It enabled me to talk about new priorities for our church in ways that would be heard and believed."

NATE STRATMAN
DIRECTOR OF FAMILY MINISTRIES
First Presbyterian, Colorado Springs, Colorado

THE PROBLEM

Research shows that 40-50 percent of students from good youth groups and families will drift from God and the church after high school. As leaders and as parents, we're not satisfied with that. We suspect you're not either.

THE RESPONSE

In our study of over 500 youth group graduates, we uncovered three main shifts that are needed to help young people develop a faith that sticks. If we were sitting across from you at our favorite coffee shop, here's how we would show you the basics of Sticky Faith on a napkin:

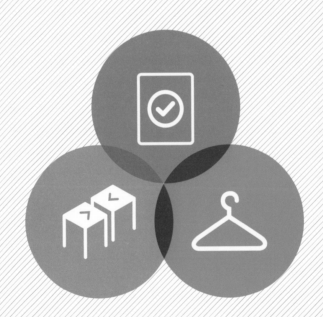

 ▶ **ADDITIONAL RESOURCES**

Download these additional media resources at stickyfaithlaunchkit.org to help you share Sticky Faith:

+ "Sticky Faith Cliff Notes 15-Minute Podcast" and "5-Minute Podcast"
+ Keynote and PowerPoint slide templates you can use in your church
+ Graphics files to create your own Sticky Faith posters, newsletters, etc.

SHIFT FROM A BEHAVIOR-BASED GOSPEL
TO A GRACE-BASED GOSPEL

When asked to describe what it means to be a Christian, most young people point to a list of behaviors. They believe God will like them better if they can follow a list of "Do's" and "Don'ts" based on keeping their sin in check. This type of faith is analogous to a jacket; it can be put on and taken off, but doesn't change what's on the inside. When students with this type of faith experience some sort of failure in high school or college, they feel like they've taken off their faith (like a jacket) and thrown it into a corner. We can help students develop a more robust understanding of the gospel—one that integrates faith into all of life and knows that Jesus is bigger than any mistake.

SHIFT FROM A TWO-TABLE CHURCH TO WELCOMING
YOUNG PEOPLE AROUND ONE FAMILY TABLE

Our research shows that intergenerational worship and relationships are linked with faith that sticks. The problem is that many of our students don't know the church at all; they only know the youth group. The better we get at youth ministry, the more we tend to segregate students, much like an adults' table and a kids' table at a family gathering. While we're *not* calling for an end to youth ministry, we *are* calling for a new approach where the whole church finds more ways to come around one table as a faith family. Ideally, each young person is surrounded by a team of five adults who consistently support and walk with him or her. We call this a new 5:1 ratio for ministry.

SHIFT FROM "DRY-CLEANER" PARENTING TO
MINISTRY PARTNERSHIP

Dry-cleaner parents drop their kids off at youth group, expecting to pick them up 90 minutes later all clean and pressed. In other words, parents have learned to outsource their kids' spiritual development to the church and its leadership. Youth leaders need to imagine new ways to partner with parents in their kids' faith formation so they are empowered and equipped to nurture faith in the family.

PRACTICE NOW! Pretend you're at lunch with Stan, the children's ministry leader at your church, and he asks, "What's this Sticky Faith thing about?" How do you respond? Grab a napkin and start sketching!

Part 4

HOW DO I BUILD THE TEAM I NEED SO I DON'T FEEL LIKE I'M DOING THIS ALONE?

▶ VIDEO
Download the 5-minute video "How do I build a team?" at stickyfaithlaunchkit.org.

We know that as a leader you're often inundated with "to-do's" and requests from all sides. We also know what it's like to think you can handle new initiatives on your own. After all, you've balanced everything so far, right?

When it comes to implementing Sticky Faith changes, that kind of thinking might hurt more than it helps. Your tendency may be either to tackle this on your own or to make it part of your regular leadership team meetings. Neither approach typically works well. The seemingly urgent priorities you face week after week as a leader tend to swallow up any important changes you might need to make.

Instead, we recommend that you designate a separate **Sticky Faith Launch Team** that will meet every three weeks or so. This team will be your key support system over the next 180 days and beyond.

DESIGNATE
A SEPARATE
STICKY FAITH
LAUNCH TEAM

MEET
THE TEAM
WILL MEET EVERY 3
WEEKS OR SO

SUPPORT
THE TEAM WILL
BE YOUR SUPPORT
SYSTEM OVER THE
NEXT 180 DAYS

Start by praying together about the hopes and dreams God has for your ministry. Then work together to assess what's going on now, formulate a plan for where you hope to go, and implement it together. We'll walk you through that process throughout Module 1.

Believe it or not, the youth pastor probably isn't the best person to follow up on progress made by this team. While you're swamped with carrying out the day-to-day ministry, designate a team member or volunteer whose job it is to hold everyone's feet to the fire to keep moving forward on big-picture changes.

Here's why. The first couple of months will go well because you're excited. But sooner or later, the mundane will catch up to you. That's when it's important to have a designated person who will follow up with others in between meetings to remind everyone to keep Sticky Faith at the forefront of their agenda. If this doesn't happen, the regular activities of life will take over and derail your efforts to make changes stick.

FROM OUR EXPERIENCE WITH OTHER CHURCHES, THE SOONER YOU PULL YOUR CHILDREN'S MINISTRY LEADERSHIP INTO THIS TEAM, THE BETTER.

 LAUNCH TIP

"We thought we understood what we were getting into when we started implementing Sticky Faith in our church. But the more we do, the larger the list gets for things we would like to do! One thing we wish we would have known beforehand is that the Sticky Faith movement really needs to have focused attention of one key leader, staff member, or volunteer. Otherwise it's not sustainable for any age-level leader to champion this cause and continue to lead his or her ministry through the change process. It's difficult to keep the movement going without someone prodding the team forward!"

NATE ROSKAM
COMMUNITY LIFE PASTOR
Nampa First Nazarene, Nampa, Idaho

WHAT NOW?

Here are a few steps to take now in order to make changes that really *stick:*

1 **CHOOSE YOUR TEAM**

Decide who will be part of your Sticky Faith Launch Team. The ideal size of this team will vary based on your context. Consider inviting core leaders from your adult volunteer team, a parent or two, a church staff member, a senior adult, and possibly a mature student leader. From our experience with other churches, the sooner you pull your children's ministry leadership into this team, the better. Moving beyond ministry silos (children's ministry, middle school ministry, high school ministry, adult ministry, etc.) is often a goal of congregations who participate in the launch process.

2 **GET IT ON THE CALENDAR**

Right away, put your meeting dates for the next few months on the calendar. Schedule them approximately every three weeks. Soon you might want to set aside a three-hour meeting, a half- or whole-day retreat, or some other intensive time to work through what you learn in your assessment (Module 1, Part 5) and begin to craft stories that communicate an emerging vision for change (Module 1, Part 6).

3 **MAKE A TASK LIST**

Make sure that at the end of each meeting, you have a clear list of tasks that will be accomplished by the next meeting.

4 **SET ACCOUNTABILITY**

Choose a volunteer who will be responsible for following up with others to make sure they accomplish their tasks in between meetings.

5 **KEEP YOUR MEETINGS ON TRACK**

The following questions can help keep you on track between meetings:

> » What has shown the most improvement since our last meeting? Where can we celebrate small victories?
> » Are there areas where we're getting stuck or where we need to reevaluate?
> » In general, does it feel like we're still on the right track?
> » What needs to be accomplished in the next three weeks? By whom?

What will you do when you first meet? Begin by giving everyone an overview of Sticky Faith (Module 1, Part 3), and then practice one or more of the assessment exercises in Module 1, Part 5.

Part 5

ASSESSING WHERE WE ARE RIGHT NOW

▶ **ADDITIONAL RESOURCES**

ONLINE SURVEY

We've created an online survey to help you—and us—measure the effectiveness of your ministry in various Sticky Faith areas both before and after your launch process. Take a few moments to complete that survey now at stickyfaithlaunchkit.org. You'll also have the opportunity to see where your church self-assesses in comparison to other churches, as well as track your growth in these areas over time.

The first thing you'll want to explore with your team is where your ministry stands *now* when it comes to Sticky Faith.

Based on the Sticky Faith overview in Part 3, how would you assess your youth ministry health right now? What's the current reality? Keep reading for a few practical steps you can take on your own or with your Launch Team (if you skipped Part 4 about assembling that team, loop back before moving on!) over the next few weeks to get a good read on where things are now, which will help you discern the path you need to take in order to get where you hope to be 180 days from now and 180 days beyond that.

One of the key lessons we've learned from Dr. Scott Cormode here at Fuller over the past few years is that *leadership begins with listening*. Your leadership should not begin with speaking or attempting to change others, but by **listening** to them.

▶ **VIDEO**

Download the 2-minute video "Listen for what?" at stickyfaithlaunchkit.org. Watch this with your team to tip off a discussion about assessing your ministry.

PRIMARILY, YOU SHOULD LISTEN FOR TWO THINGS:

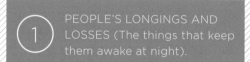

① PEOPLE'S LONGINGS AND LOSSES (The things that keep them awake at night).

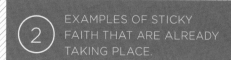

② EXAMPLES OF STICKY FAITH THAT ARE ALREADY TAKING PLACE.

1   For a more detailed explanation of longings, losses, and how Christian leaders can better relate theology to the things that keep people awake at night, see *Making Spiritual Sense: Christian Leaders as Spiritual Interpreters* by Scott Cormode.

INVESTIGATE WITH YOUR TEAM

Take a look at the following ideas to help your team listen in ways that help assess your current ministry based on the three core findings of Sticky Faith we described in Module 1, Part 3:

 ASSESS STUDENTS' UNDERSTANDING OF THE GOSPEL.

Sit down with a group of young people and ask them to describe what it means to be a Christian. Listen carefully and take notes on what you hear (or jot down notes immediately afterward). You and your leadership team could get together with students or make this a small group discussion exercise. The key is that you come back together and formulate a clear picture of how your students understand the gospel right now.

 ASSESS INTERGENERATIONAL CONNECTIONS.

Consider making an "intergenerational map" of your church campus. This map helps you to understand where students spend time and to identify where there are opportunities for them to interact more with adults. Detailed instructions can be found in the handout titled **"Creating an Intergenerational Map of Your Church Campus"** available for download at stickyfaithlaunchkit.org. Beyond church space, look for intergenerational programmatic and relational connections that are already occurring. What is it that seems to spark or fuel these connections? What stories have you heard?

 ASSESS PARTNERSHIP WITH PARENTS.

A. MAKE APPOINTMENTS

Meet one-on-one with a handful of parents in your ministry over coffee or a meal. Ask them some of the following questions (and be ready to graciously hear the answers):

» What do you think is going well in our youth ministry?
» What are we doing well when it comes to supporting you and other parents?
» How could we grow as a ministry?
» What ideas do you have for how we could better partner with parents?
» What are some of your biggest parenting questions these days?

B. COMPILE YOUR FINDINGS INTO A SUMMARY YOU CAN SHARE WITH YOUR TEAM

With your leadership team, make a list of all of the programs and structures that make up your youth ministry. Walk through that list and assess which items partner with parents well and which do not, and brainstorm new ideas for moving toward partnership. (Note that Module 3 is overflowing with tested ideas and tools for engaging parents, so consider this assessment a first step, not a time to solidify any changes.)

ASSESSING THE CURRENT STATE OF YOUR YOUTH MINISTRY IS BOTH AN ART AND A SCIENCE. THERE'S NO ONE-SIZE-FITS-ALL APPROACH. WHILE THESE EXERCISES PROVIDE SOME IDEAS TO GET STARTED, FEEL FREE TO COME UP WITH YOUR OWN ASSESSMENT THAT FITS YOUR CONTEXT!

WHAT NOW?

Process your findings as a team from these three categories. Arm yourselves with butcher paper and markers, and assign someone to capture words and images from the group's learning. Be sure to start with the positive before moving into areas of growth. It's helpful to set a clear start and end time for this conversation, and assign a timekeeper to announce the halfway point and a final fifteen-minute warning. At that point you can decide whether you need to set another meeting to process your findings further before moving on.

▶ **INSTRUCTIONAL NOTE**
GOALS

The goals of the assessment process are awareness and understanding, not developing concrete plans. You'll get to that in Parts 6-8 of this module, and Modules 2-4 will give you even more tools.

Use the following questions as a guide for your assessment process. Feel free to adapt or create some questions of your own based on your context.

 ▶ **HANDOUT**
ASSESSING OUR CHURCH

Available to the right, as well as for download at stickyfaithlaunchkit.org. For this and other handouts, feel free to make as many copies as you'd like for your team. We have uploaded an 8.5x11 version of each handout so that you can easily print and photocopy them for your ministry.

In order to implement Sticky Faith, you're eventually going to ask people to make some changes. If you change people's expectations too slowly, nothing happens. If you change expectations too quickly, it can cause panic or even a mutiny. **Listening helps you to understand those you lead and to respect how quickly (or slowly) changes should be introduced.** We'll loop back to this in Module 4, Part 2.

 ▶ **HANDOUT**
CREATING AN INTERGENERATIONAL MAP OF YOUR CHURCH CAMPUS
Available for download at stickyfaithlaunchkit.org.

ASSESSING OUR CHURCH

Based on what we've learned, what can we celebrate? What's going right in our ministry?

How do students at our church seem to understand the gospel? What adjustments do we need to make in our teaching and our community in order to nurture an environment of grace?

How well are we doing at facilitating intergenerational ministry? How could we grow?

What are parents' expectations of our youth ministry? What could we do to improve our partnership with parents?

What are some of the "longings and losses" we are hearing from our congregation as we have these conversations? What can we learn from them? What are some of our own longings and losses we experience related to our youth ministry and our whole church? What can we learn from those?

Taking these areas into account, how far are we now from where we want our youth ministry to go? Why?

Think of a change we would like to make in our ministry. What would be our natural first step toward making that change? To whom else should we be listening before we make any concrete plans?

What—or who—are positive forces in bringing about change in our youth ministry and church?

What do we anticipate will be some of the major obstacles to change?

Part 6

HOW DO WE DEVELOP AND COMMUNICATE A VISION FOR CHANGE?

▶ **INSTRUCTIONAL NOTE**
You might want to set aside a three-hour meeting, a half- or whole-day retreat, or some other intensive time to tackle Part 6 as a Launch Team.

▶ **VIDEO**
Download the 5-minute video "How do I communicate the Sticky Faith vision to others?" at stickyfaithlaunchkit.org. Watch this video with your Launch Team to spark a discussion about forming and sharing a new Sticky Faith vision.

HOW DO YOU DEFINE VISION?

We've heard dozens of definitions for the term "vision," few of which we can remember. By contrast, the definition given by our Fuller colleague Scott Cormode has captured our imaginations and the imaginations of hundreds of churches. Scott defines vision as "a shared story of future hope."

VISION IS A SHARED STORY OF FUTURE HOPE.

This understanding of vision is about inviting people to participate in a new story that is created by weaving together your story, my story, and the biblical story. This is the reason listening is so important. If you haven't listened to those you lead, you won't know what is important to them and won't be able to connect them to your vision.

By weaving your story and another person's story with the biblical story, you're inviting that person into something that's much bigger than your personal vision. You're not just asking them to trust you; you're asking them to trust God.

Once you capture this new story, invite people to *live into* it. As they do, they will take the new language that you've given them and use it to organize their lives. They will begin to see the language and new ideas in places they had not expected. Over time, people will take this new story and make it their own.

ONCE YOU FIND
A GOOD STORY
ABOUT WHAT GOD
IS ALREADY DOING,
TELL IT EVERY
OPPORTUNITY
YOU GET.

▶ **VIDEO**

Download the 4-minute video "Where do I find stories to introduce some-thing new?" to watch with your team at this point in the discussion, especial-ly if you need a practical example of what this looks like.

To introduce something new, the best place to start is with what's *not new*—with peo-ple's longings and hopes. For example, most parents want their kids to have the same commitment to Jesus that they have. To create shared stories of future hope, start by listening for these longings. Also listen for stories that are already taking place in your congregation that are examples of Sticky Faith.

▶ **VIDEO**

If you can handle it, here's one more video to help round out this critical topic with another story from a Sticky Faith church! Download the 4-minute video "What should I do once I find a good story?" from stickyfaithlaunchkit.org.

Once you find a good story about what God is already doing, tell it every opportuni-ty you get. This can be at a church meeting, in a conversation with a parent, or when someone asks you what's going on in your youth ministry. Create multiple lengths of the story so you can tell it in a variety of settings. **Tell it enough that every person in the church can tell it.** This story will give people a glimpse of what is possible. It is something that you're inviting them to imagine and even recreate on their own terms. When they do this, they participate in a shared story of future hope. Who wouldn't want to do that?

WHAT NOW?

Now it's time to practice! As a team, work together to develop a story of Sticky Faith that best communicates your vision.

 COMPILE STORIES

First, tell a few true stories from your congregation that you think illustrate your understanding of Sticky Faith, and write them down. (Recall some of the stories you might have heard as a team in Module 1, Part 5).

 SELECT A STORY

Agree together on one of these stories (for now) that you want to refine and share with others to help communicate your vision—your shared story of future hope.

 FIND OPPORTUNITIES

Next, have each person write out every opportunity you'll have over the next week to share this story. This might include a staff meeting, dinner with a student's family, a small group gathering, or a chance meeting with your lead pastor in the hallway. Talk about what version of the story you would share in each of these settings and how the story leads into a conversation about Sticky Faith. You'll all want to be prepared with a length that will fit any situation.

 SHARE

Take a few weeks and share the story as much as possible. After that time, come back together and talk about how it went. Use the **"Telling shared stories of future hope: How'd it go?"** handout to lead your discussion. You might want to modify the story based on what you learn. You might also want to create a few imaginary stories of what the future might look like—stories of students, families, or the whole congregation. Consider doing this exercise with your entire youth ministry volunteer team and see what stories emerge (Module 2, Part 3 provides tools for a team training session on this). Continue to share stories until everyone in your church catches the vision and can retell your stories!

 ▶ **HANDOUT**
TELLING SHARED STORIES OF FUTURE HOPE: HOW'D IT GO?
Available to the right, as well as online.

TELLING SHARED STORIES OF FUTURE HOPE: HOW'D IT GO?

What kinds of reactions did you get when you shared the story?

What do we make of those reactions? What can we learn from them?

How well can we articulate the ministry changes this story represents? If the changes aren't clear, is there another story that captures our hope more vividly?

For those who were excited about the vision, how could we invite them to participate in moving this vision forward?

What can we do to ensure we communicate our story to everyone in the congregation?

What are some small changes we can begin to make that would move us toward the Sticky Faith vision captured in the story? What do you think our next steps should be?

WE USUALLY ASK
LEADERS TO IMAGINE
HOW MUCH THEY
THINK THEY NEED TO
COMMUNICATE ABOUT
A CHANGE, AND THEN
DOUBLE IT.

LAUNCH TIP

When we asked churches who had been through our cohort process what they wish they would have done differently, the most common responses centered around wishing they had communicated earlier, more often, and more broadly to parents and the congregation, and by telling stories more clearly. Buy-in can't happen without loads of communication. In fact, we usually ask leaders to imagine how much they *think* they need to communicate about a change, and then *double* it.

RESOURCES FOR CREATING AND SHARING VISION STORIES:

"BUILDING YOUR COMPANY'S VISION"
By Jim Collins and Jerry Porras
A *Harvard Business Review* article that explains the importance of a vision, as well as how to build one.

http://hbr.org/1996/09/building-your-companys-vision/ar/1

"TWO STICKY SENIORS"
A video by Lars Rood that tells the Sticky Faith stories of two students
http://fulleryouthinstitute.org/2010/12/two-sticky-seniors/

TEACHING THROUGH THE ART OF STORYTELLING:
CREATING FICTIONAL STORIES THAT ILLUSTRATE THE MESSAGE OF JESUS
By Jon Huckins

SHAPED BY THE STORY:
HELPING STUDENTS ENCOUNTER GOD IN A NEW WAY
By Michael Novelli

Part 7

NOW, HOW DO WE ACTUALLY GET PEOPLE TO CHANGE?

It's not news that most churches seem full of people who are afraid of change. You can probably create a sizeable list of suspects who fit that description in your church.

> ## WHAT WE'RE MISSING, THOUGH, IS THAT THEIR FEAR ISN'T PRIMARILY ABOUT *CHANGE;* IT'S ABOUT *LOSS*. PEOPLE DON'T ACTUALLY RESIST CHANGE; THEY RESIST LOSS.[1]

▶ **VIDEO**

Don't believe us? Download the 3-minute video "Why are people afraid of change?" You'll probably want to share it with your Launch Team too.

The Sticky Faith changes you're going to ask people to make will cost them something. **As a leader, part of your role is to figure out that cost.** For example, many of the parents in your church may have had a great experience in youth group when they were teenagers, and they now want to replicate that exact same experience for their own son or daughter. If you're introducing a different approach to youth ministry, you're asking them to give up their expectation of what youth ministry *should be*. That's a huge loss!

HOW SHOULD WE RESPOND WHEN THOSE FEARS FLARE UP?

▶ **VIDEO**

Download the 3-minute video "How should I respond to people's fear of change?" for a few practical tips for how to handle the fear of change and loss you'll likely encounter.

---

1   This phrase and much of the content in this section are borrowed from our Fuller colleague Dr. Scott Cormode.

The leader and team's job is to anticipate the losses involved and prepare a response. This means that you must be proactive in listening to those you lead, so that you'll be able to anticipate how or when they might feel loss. Once you're aware of this, meet with these people (maybe more than once) and give them a vision of what can be possible if the change is made. Once they begin to understand your vision, they'll have a new framework to experience the change not as loss, but as hope.

WHAT NOW?

To the right is a chart to help you and your team begin to anticipate losses that might be associated with changes you hope to make. The first four rows are examples of common changes that many people go through, as well as some of the losses associated with each change. The next three rows are left blank for you and your team to fill in.

At your next Launch Team meeting, distribute copies of this chart. As a group, discuss each of the examples of change in the left column and come up with other losses that might be associated with each change. Next, give everyone time (on their own) to think of two to four changes your youth ministry needs to make and the losses that might be associated with each change. Then come back together as a group and discuss your findings based on the reflection questions on the handout.

▶ **HANDOUT** $\longrightarrow$
NAVIGATING CHANGE AND LOSS
Available to the right, as well as online.

NAVIGATING CHANGE AND LOSS

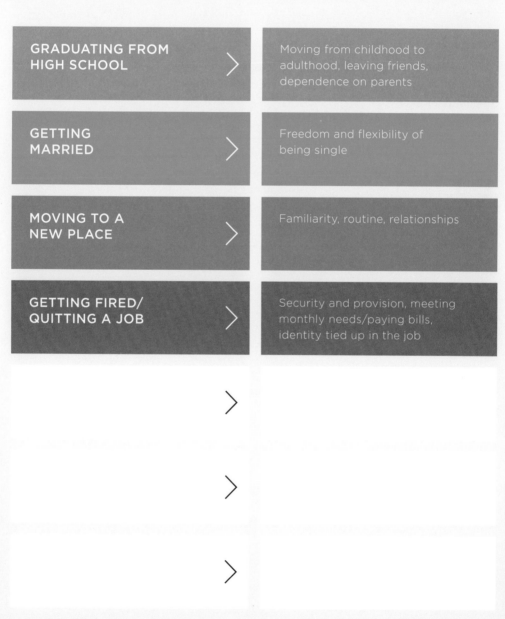

| GRADUATING FROM HIGH SCHOOL ⟩ | Moving from childhood to adulthood, leaving friends, dependence on parents |

| GETTING MARRIED ⟩ | Freedom and flexibility of being single |

| MOVING TO A NEW PLACE ⟩ | Familiarity, routine, relationships |

| GETTING FIRED/ QUITTING A JOB ⟩ | Security and provision, meeting monthly needs/paying bills, identity tied up in the job |

DEBRIEFING QUESTIONS

What was surprising about this exercise? What's one new insight this exercise has for our discussion of change?

What are the changes our ministry might need to make, and what are the losses associated with each of those changes?

Who will be experiencing those losses? Who else do we need to be talking with about this?

What can we do to be proactive in responding to the losses? Who will do this?

How does this relate to vision and to the stories we have been telling (see Module 1, Part 6)?

Based on all that we're learning, what ideas do we have about the next steps we should take? What experiments could help us test the readiness of our ministry or whole congregation for change?

 ▶ **ADDITIONAL RESOURCES**
For additional resources to help you lead change in the midst of resistance see a list of links at stickyfaithlaunchkit.org.

THE LEADER AND TEAM'S JOB IS TO ANTICIPATE THE LOSSES INVOLVED AND PREPARE A RESPONSE.

Part 8

DEVELOPING A BREAK-THROUGH PLAN

Now that you've assembled a team, nurtured a vision, and considered the losses associated with possible changes, you might be ready to develop a Breakthrough Plan . . . or you might want to crawl into a fetal position for a few days and take slow, cleansing breaths. That's okay too. Once you emerge from that place, *then* you might be ready.

We say "might" because we don't really know you or your church. In our experience, some churches need to lay quite a bit more groundwork prior to developing a solid plan. Other churches are able to utilize this plan to lay that groundwork, and then they can lead into next-level changes. We invite you to consider with your Launch Team whether you're ready for this step now or whether you should do some further work first and loop back to this later.

WRITING YOUR BREAKTHROUGH PLAN

Below you will find a template for developing your own Breakthrough Plan with your team. While ideally it will represent collaborative work, you will probably find it easiest to assign one person (you or someone else) to be the point person to write the plan. Some churches find the template below really helpful, while others adapt it for their context or work on goal setting based on a structure that works more naturally in their ministry.

That said, we also see churches that fail to develop a breakthrough plan at all. Often these churches have a hard time keeping focus and momentum toward the changes they hope to see. We don't want that to happen to your team, so please set aside some focused time to tackle the questions and charts below, working through the details with your Launch Team based on your context.

▶ **ADDITIONAL RESOURCES**

We've included an editable Microsoft Word Document version of this Breakthrough Plan template at stickyfaithlaunchkit.org that you can download to easily adapt and complete for your ministry.

According to Dr. Scott Cormode, vision is a "shared story of future hope." Given this definition, write two stories of specific teenagers in your church that capture your vision for Sticky Faith. Ideally these stories will be cast one or two years from now.

Story #1:

Story #2:

 Reflecting on these stories and the conversations you've been having with your Sticky Faith Launch Team over the past few months, what are the two or three Sticky Faith change areas that are most important for you to focus on? (e.g., intergenerational relationships, partnering with parents, embracing doubts, transitions, moving beyond the "gospel of sin management").

 ▶ **ADDITIONAL RESOURCES**
If you feel like you need more content prior to contextualizing change areas, please check out *Sticky Faith: Youth Worker Edition* and additional resources at stickyfaith.org. You also might want to check out Modules 3 and 4 in this Launch Kit for more specific ideas related to engaging parents and the broader church.

 How are these change areas linked to who you already are and how God has already shaped you as a church/ministry? In other words, where are signs of hope that these changes are already happening?

Who are the people you will need to work with in order to make these changes possible? (These are the individuals/groups of people who will be affected by your vision, who need to be involved in this process, or who can help the vision be implemented as you move forward.) What are some of the potential losses these people or groups might experience as a result of the proposed changes, and how will you respond to their fears and losses?

5 Now it's time to move from intentions to tangible, measurable plans. *The following is one way to put together such a plan. If it's not helpful to you or if there's another format you'd like to follow, you can do so. What is most important is that you have a clear plan.* The tables below are for you to write out your plan for each change area. Follow these steps to complete each table:

a. At the top of the table, name the specific change.

b. In the next section, list three or four desired outcomes (goals) you'd like to see in this change area. Be as specific as possible.

c. In the far left column, list the people who will need to be involved in the change (e.g., students, parents, youth ministry team, overall church, senior pastor, elders). List one group of people in each row.

d. The next three columns are three important categories related to change (the order is not important, but paying attention to these categories will help you maintain focus and gain momentum):
    » EDUCATION:
       How will people be educated about the need for the change?
    » ENCOURAGEMENT:
       How will people be encouraged to make the change?
    » EXPOSURE:
       How will people be exposed to the change (in small or large pieces)?

Write down the ways you will educate, encourage, and expose each group of people to the change.

e. At the bottom of each Education, Encouragement, and Exposure box, list a point person and target date for the item listed (e.g., Courtney by December 1). By naming a point person, you are both setting up an accountability structure and committing to empower this person (as the best-qualified person on your team) to deliver this part of the plan.

f. Once you've completed the table, repeat the process for each of your change areas.

CHANGE AREA #1

DESIRED OUTCOMES:

1.

2.

3.

PEOPLE
WHO NEEDS TO BE INVOLVED

EDUCATION
HOW THESE PEOPLE WILL BE
EDUCATED ABOUT THE NEED
FOR CHANGE

TARGET DATE:
POINT PERSON:

TARGET DATE:
POINT PERSON:

TARGET DATE:
POINT PERSON:

TARGET DATE:
POINT PERSON:

ENCOURAGEMENT
HOW THESE PEOPLE WILL BE
ENCOURAGED TO MAKE THE CHANGE

EXPOSURE
HOW THESE PEOPLE WILL BE
EXPOSED TO THE CHANGE IN SMALL
OR LARGE PIECES

TARGET DATE:
POINT PERSON:

TARGET DATE:
POINT PERSON:

TARGET DATE:
POINT PERSON:

TARGET DATE:
POINT PERSON:

TARGET DATE:
POINT PERSON:

TARGET DATE:
POINT PERSON:

TARGET DATE:
POINT PERSON:

TARGET DATE:
POINT PERSON:

CHANGE AREA **#2**

DESIRED OUTCOMES:

1.
2.
3.

PEOPLE
WHO NEEDS TO BE INVOLVED

EDUCATION
HOW THESE PEOPLE WILL BE
EDUCATED ABOUT THE NEED
FOR CHANGE

TARGET DATE:
POINT PERSON:

TARGET DATE:
POINT PERSON:

TARGET DATE:
POINT PERSON:

TARGET DATE:
POINT PERSON:

ENCOURAGEMENT
HOW THESE PEOPLE WILL BE
ENCOURAGED TO MAKE THE CHANGE

EXPOSURE
HOW THESE PEOPLE WILL BE
EXPOSED TO THE CHANGE IN SMALL
OR LARGE PIECES

TARGET DATE:
POINT PERSON:

TARGET DATE:
POINT PERSON:

TARGET DATE:
POINT PERSON:

TARGET DATE:
POINT PERSON:

TARGET DATE:
POINT PERSON:

TARGET DATE:
POINT PERSON:

TARGET DATE:
POINT PERSON:

TARGET DATE:
POINT PERSON:

CHANGE AREA #3

DESIRED OUTCOMES:

1.
2.
3.

PEOPLE
WHO NEEDS TO BE INVOLVED

EDUCATION
HOW THESE PEOPLE WILL BE
EDUCATED ABOUT THE NEED
FOR CHANGE

TARGET DATE:
POINT PERSON:

TARGET DATE:
POINT PERSON:

TARGET DATE:
POINT PERSON:

TARGET DATE:
POINT PERSON:

ENCOURAGEMENT
HOW THESE PEOPLE WILL BE
ENCOURAGED TO MAKE THE CHANGE

EXPOSURE
HOW THESE PEOPLE WILL BE
EXPOSED TO THE CHANGE IN SMALL
OR LARGE PIECES

TARGET DATE:
POINT PERSON:

TARGET DATE:
POINT PERSON:

TARGET DATE:
POINT PERSON:

TARGET DATE:
POINT PERSON:

TARGET DATE:
POINT PERSON:

TARGET DATE:
POINT PERSON:

TARGET DATE:
POINT PERSON:

TARGET DATE:
POINT PERSON:

6   How do you plan to give these changes focused attention? (List the people who will be involved in your Launch Team, the frequency of your meetings, and what will be done during and in between meetings.)

7   At this point, what could prevent you from realizing your vision? What might hinder the plan? How will you keep from getting distracted?

▶ **ADDITIONAL RESOURCES**

SHARE YOUR PLAN!

Want to see a sample of a completed Breakthrough Plan? Want feedback from other leaders on your plan? Want to crowdsource ideas for implementing Sticky Faith? Want specialized consulting from a trained Sticky Faith coach based on your plan? Visit stickyfaithlaunchkit.org for any or all of these services.

THIS IS SO MUCH WORK. HOW DO WE KNOW WHEN WE'RE READY TO LAUNCH?

We can't give you a simple answer to this question. The goal of this module has been to help you consider all the groundwork you should do in order to get ready to launch, and we've given you the tools you need for the first few months of your launch. It's also possible you will get to this point and determine that you need to call a "hold."

Back to our shuttle launch analogy, a **built-in hold** is a period in a launch countdown where the countdown clock is stopped. It might be for a few moments or a few hours. You might need to make a critical decision, complete a safety checklist, or put a full pause on the mission.[1] If you sense the Lord nudging you to push "hold" for a few weeks, months, or even longer, please do so. In a process like this, rushing rarely pays off.

---

1   For NASA geeks, see http://en.wikipedia.org/wiki/Built-in_hold.

Part 9

HOW CAN WE KEEP UP MOMENTUM?

LAUNCH TIP

"This process was most effective because as a team we were all focused on one issue at a time."

TIM GALLEHER
PASTOR OF YOUTH AND FAMILY MINISTRIES
Saratoga Federated Church, Saratoga, California

It doesn't take long to figure out that momentum is crucial in youth ministry. Whether you're herding middle schoolers at an event or guiding your volunteer team at a meeting, you need some kind of energy to keep everyone moving forward.

Momentum may seem elusive at times, but you certainly know when you've lost it. Eyes glaze over, people stop showing up, or no one appears to know what next steps to take. When you implement new sticky strategies—especially those that require a shift in church culture—great momentum is required to stay on track.

SO HOW DO WE CREATE AND SUSTAIN MOMENTUM IN THE MIDST OF MAKING CRUCIAL CHANGES?

Below you'll find elements that have proven to be helpful companions for other leaders on the path toward implementing sustainable change.[1]

---

[1]   Special thanks to Nate Stratman from First Presbyterian Church of Colorado Springs for contributing these insights.

PACE YOURSELVES

Some congregations find Sticky Faith to be so exciting that they leap forward with gusto. Like racehorses eager to reach the finish line, they launch out of the gates in a dead sprint full of new ideas and programmatic solutions. This sprint ends up resembling something like a huge sugar rush followed by a hard crash.

You'll do well to pay close attention to your pace. You need time to contextualize the Sticky Faith philosophy before trying to implement change, and your congregation can get easily overwhelmed with facts and dreams that they don't have time to digest. Initiatives like creating more intergenerational experiences or partnering more intentionally with families often represent huge cultural shifts within a congregation's DNA. This kind of shift will demand a healthy (and often slower-than-you'd-like) pace.

IDENTIFY CHAMPIONS AND CHEERLEADERS

On its own, Sticky Faith research will likely resound with many people in your church. Most churches want to care for the younger generations, but often they don't know how. Some of your older members will find new purpose in the family of God as you share about the importance of intergenerational connections. Some of your parents will get excited about deeper partnership. Tap into these early adapters as champions and cheerleaders for the new movement you're guiding within your congregation. Equip them with talking points and stories for communicating the vision to groups with whom they're naturally connected.

Similarly, part of the role of your Launch Team is going to be championing Sticky Faith across the congregation. During these first 180 days, try to gain an audience with every subgroup of your church, from the pulpit to the preschool parents. Here's how our friend Nate Stratman did this within his church in Colorado Springs:

> I went on tour around the groups within our church. In each setting I would share a stat, a story, and a dream. For example, I would share Sticky Faith research that shows the problem of completely segregating our church based on age. Then I would tell a story of a kid named Josh whose dad abandoned him in middle school. He dreams of going fishing, but there is nobody in his life who knows how or who wants to take him.
>
> Finally, I shared this dream: "What if there were five men in this church who would be willing to take Josh fishing?" By presenting the crisis and then a story that puts flesh on the crisis, I have the opportunity to show others in our church how they can easily make a difference in a young person's life by responding in tangible ways. We encourage our team to keep stories like these handy so we can help our congregation see how they can participate in what God is doing through Sticky Faith.

▶ **INSTRUCTIONAL NOTE**
LIKE THIS IDEA?
In Module 4, Part 3 we've given you tools to create your own "Sticky Faith Tour" through your congregation!

CHECK YOUR GUT

This one is simple and vital. As your team regularly gathers, share a story or two of how you've seen Sticky Faith lived out in your context. Then ask, "Do we still believe this is the right emphasis for our church for right now?" The gut check is a quick way to make sure everyone is "all in" and pushing in the same direction. The team may want to discuss some needed tweaks to your plan. But by asking if you're still on the right track, you help maintain momentum by reminding the team of your focus and its rewards.

Taking this to the level of your everyday work, clearly naming Sticky Faith vision and outcomes makes it clearer what to say "yes" and "no" to on a day-to-day basis. It becomes the gut check you need when faced with competing priorities.

BRING IN FRESH VOICES

Recruiting a Launch Team that is committed to making your church sticky may not be difficult initially, but maintaining a vibrant team over time can be challenging. You might find that you occasionally need to add new excited people to your team while letting others rotate off and take a break. This keeps energy high and ideas fresh. It's important to remind one another that you aren't building a club, but rather participating in a movement with huge eternal significance. It will take time, and it will likely take more than just a few committed leaders.

WHAT NOW?

Great companies generally have great research and design (R&D) teams. As you continue to build and lead your Launch Team, you might think of it in terms of a spiritual R&D team. This team assesses the cultural shifts needed in the church and then they design and implement an approach.

A good R&D team never stops researching and designing, nor should your Sticky Faith implementation team. It is important that you feel the freedom to risk, experiment, fail, and then try again. You will try something that you think might bless families and learn that it actually causes great stress. Be willing to go back to the drawing board, reevaluate, and launch again. Over time, you're likely to see a culture shift beginning to take place as some of those changes take root in your church.

HOW WE RECOMMEND YOU MOVE FORWARD FROM HERE

Each module in this series is designed to be a reference point you can return to over and over again throughout your launch process. We asked you to start with Module 1, but from here you can jump around among Modules 2-4 as needed. They are meant to be practical tools to help you equip your broader volunteer team, parents, and the entire church to invest in Sticky Faith. In Module 4 you'll also find some more strategic questions your Launch Team may want to consider together, including:

» How fast can I make changes?
» How can I help my senior pastor understand what needs to change?
» How do I change the way people think about the mission of youth ministry?

If you feel like you need to address those questions on the sooner side, jump right on over to Module 4 as a next step. If you'd rather tackle your parent engagement strategy, see Module 3. You get the idea. Make this your own journey. Hopefully your Breakthrough Plan will inform your selection and timing through the modules. But more importantly, we hope you'll listen to the prompting of the Holy Spirit to guide your ministry step by step into the future. We believe this launch process has a lot of merit, but our confidence in the process is tempered by a deep sense that God leads each church in unique and sometimes unpredictable ways.

As you experiment, please keep in touch! Our team is ready to interact with you on stickyfaithlaunchkit.org. We also invite you to share stories online at stickyfaith.org/stories to encourage and inspire other leaders and churches to take steps toward Sticky Faith!

A GOOD R&D TEAM NEVER STOPS RESEARCHING AND DESIGNING, NOR SHOULD YOUR STICKY FAITH IMPLEMENTATION TEAM. IT IS IMPORTANT THAT YOU FEEL THE FREEDOM TO RISK, EXPERIMENT, FAIL, AND THEN TRY AGAIN.

MODULE 02

VOLUNTEER TRAINING

Part 1

HOW CAN I CREATE A TRAINING RHYTHM THAT WORKS FOR OUR MINISTRY AND OUR VOLUNTEERS?

GETTING THE WHOLE TEAM ON BOARD

In Module 1, Part 4, we encouraged you to build a Launch Team. Hopefully you're working with that team right now to develop and implement Sticky Faith changes based on a Breakthrough Plan you've created together (see Module 1, Part 8). But depending on the size of your ministry, the Launch Team is likely not your whole volunteer team. This module was written to help you intentionally train the rest of your volunteers, including small group leaders, Sunday school teachers, program ministry helpers, retreat counselors, mentors, and anyone else who serves in ministry to young people. You might even want to combine your children and youth ministry teams for these sessions, or you could use the content in both groups separately, making tweaks based on the ministry context. Also, while we use the word "volunteer" a lot in these outlines, if you have a larger paid staff team, by all means include them and adapt your language!

First things first: You need a training rhythm.

Helping your volunteer team understand and implement Sticky Faith in your church will take time. Move too fast, and they'll feel lost and discouraged. Move too slow, and they'll feel bored and lose interest. The right rhythm is one that **values their time** (they're volunteers, after all), **creates consistency,** and yet **maintains flexibility.**

Your team's rhythm will certainly vary based on your context, but start by considering what you're already doing and how well it meets your goals as well as volunteers' needs. Meeting weekly might help you make faster progress, but the increased time requirement could be too much for your volunteers. On the other hand, meeting once a quarter likely won't create the consistency or momentum that you need, especially in this season of change.

We've incorporated six training sessions into the Launch Kit, so we'd recommend meeting about once per month with the broader volunteer team in order to create both a manageable commitment and a consistent pace. If you already have a training event (like a retreat for volunteers) or an established training schedule built into your ministry culture, you could consider how to customize these six sessions to fit.

In most sessions we've also included bonus ideas and exercises. Depending on how much time you have available, you might be able to work these into your meetings. But we're imagining you might loop back to these exercises at future meetings as follow-ups to continue to process the content. **That means you are holding six to twelve months of volunteer training in your hands!**

Whatever rhythm you develop, make sure to invite your volunteer team to make an initial commitment to the training meetings. The best way to go about this is by personal invitation. If possible, talk to each volunteer in person, share your vision for the training rhythm, and clearly explain the commitment expected.

If you don't have a training schedule built into your ministry already, you'll have to be diligent about reminding volunteers about upcoming meetings. Nothing is more of a barrier to this process than poor attendance at the trainings. If you find yourself hosting a poorly attended meeting, you'll face tough questions like, "Do I move forward and leave those who are absent behind?" or, "Do I postpone and send the message that meetings aren't important?" It's a tough place to be, and being proactive in inviting volunteers and getting RSVPs will go a long way toward helping you create a healthy training culture.

▶ **ADDITIONAL RESOURCES**

DOUBLE-DIP TO MAXIMIZE YOUR IMPACT

In Module 3, Part 2, we've created a whole set of fourteen emails you can send to parents on Sticky Faith topics. (Yes, we actually wrote them for you! You're welcome.) There are all kinds of reasons volunteers should be on your parent email list anyway, but just in case they aren't, now is the time to add them. Email communication can be one aspect of your ongoing volunteer training plan, and if you're already helping parents digest Sticky Faith bite by bite, why not welcome volunteers to that email feast?

---

45 ━━━━━━━━━━━━━━━━━━━━━━━━━ **90**

SET A RHYTHM FOR EACH MEETING

One key to a good training meeting is to ensure the content matches the length of the gathering. We've written the Launch Kit training sessions to span between forty-five and ninety minutes, depending on the size of the group, the context, and your personal style. If sessions are much shorter than forty-five minutes, the pace will be too quick and the volunteers might feel like it was

> WE'VE WRITTEN THE LAUNCH KIT TRAINING SESSIONS TO SPAN BETWEEN FORTY-FIVE AND NINETY MINUTES.

a waste of their time. If the sessions last longer than ninety minutes, you run the risk of volunteers feeling either bored or over-committed. You also may want to use half of a ninety-minute meeting to do the training exercise, and the remaining half for ministry planning and logistics.

CONSIDER THE COST OF THE VOLUNTEERS' TIME:

TRADE OFFS

If a person has three hours a week to give to your ministry and most of it is spent at your weekly program and at this meeting, they won't be spending time with students or going to any of their sporting events or extracurricular activities that week.

PACING

Be careful not to schedule meetings the same week as other large time requirements, like events, camps, trips, or retreats.

COMMUNICATION

Communicate through creative planning and strong execution that the meetings are important and that you value your volunteers' time. Create and facilitate an experience so good that volunteers walk out of your session confident that it was a wise use of their time. If you're not particularly skilled at group facilitation or timekeeping, ask other team members to help you or to lead portions for you.

EACH SESSION HAS FIVE PARTS TO HELP YOU MOVE THROUGH THE MEETING AND TO KEEP YOURSELF FOCUSED AND ORGANIZED. YOU'LL SEE IN THE SESSIONS THAT OUR EMPHASIS IS NOT ON WHAT YOU SHOULD SAY, BUT ON WHAT IS MOST IMPORTANT TO THE TRAINING SESSION.

THE PROBLEM

THE VISION

**POSSIBLE
SOLUTIONS**

**PRACTICAL
NEXT STEPS**

**REFLECTION
+ PRAYER**

It's also important that training sessions include variety. Sixty minutes of lecture is never a great training method, but neither is a meeting that only includes discussion. The training sessions in this Launch Kit are designed so that your meetings can include a variety of elements to help your volunteers learn and challenge them to take the next steps. The sessions aren't completely scripted—you'll have to fit them to your volunteers, your Breakthrough Plan, and your church community.

Each session has five parts to help you move through the meeting and to keep yourself focused and organized. You'll see in the sessions that our emphasis is not on what you should say, but on what is most important to the training session. You'll need to translate what's important into language and experiences your volunteers will understand.

1. THE PROBLEM

The first is a reminder of the problem. Without rooting Sticky Faith in a real problem—that young people are walking away from faith—we run the risk of it seeming like just another youth ministry model in a long list of the latest-and-greatest ideas. Your Sticky Faith Breakthrough Plan is your church's solution to the problem of faith that isn't sticking.

2. THE VISION

Next, always take a moment to recast your vision. Use the work you did with your Launch Team in creating your Breakthrough Plan to help you. What do you hope to see in your students? What do you hope to see in your church? Paint that picture for your volunteers each time you train, and share new stories of future hope as they emerge. Your goal is that by the end of your trainings, every volunteer believes in and can clearly articulate the problem, the vision, and their role in the Breakthrough Plan.

▶ INSTRUCTIONAL NOTE

This process only works if you have a clear understanding of the problem, your vision, and your Breakthrough Plan. Head back to Module 1, Parts 3-8 for a refresher as needed.

3. POSSIBLE SOLUTIONS

Third, explore possible solutions to the problem. As you've learned, there isn't one clear-cut, silver bullet solution to building Sticky Faith in students. However, our research, coupled with our in-depth work with churches from around North America, has produced some tangible strategies to help nurture lifelong faith. During each of the following chapters in this module, we've put together a training session based on the most salient strategies. The solution section is where you'll find the main content of each session.

MAKE SURE EVERY SESSION ANSWERS YOUR VOLUNTEERS' MAIN QUESTION:

"WHAT SHOULD I DO AS A RESULT OF THIS TRAINING?"

4. PRACTICAL NEXT STEPS

The fourth part is vital to any successful meeting rhythm: developing intensely practical next steps. Remember that these trainings are for volunteers—the people in your ministry who work directly with students and have real relationships with them. A training session is only helpful if it gives them something different to *do* the next time they see their students.

5. REFLECT + PRAY

Finally, you'll always want to include a reflection and prayer exercise in your meetings. This process of change isn't just about the young people you serve, it's about all of you changing and growing together. You will all be personally challenged, and your volunteers will need some space to reflect. None of this change can happen without the wisdom, courage, and perseverance that come from God.

HERE'S A PRAYER YOU CAN PRAY RIGHT NOW:

God, give me wisdom to discern the right path for our volunteers and students.
Give me courage to invite others to see the vision you've shown us so far.
Give me perseverance when I face resistance or barriers.
Your will be done, on earth as it is in heaven. Amen.

LAUNCH TIP

Want to give your team more to chew on? Consider reinforcing the theme of the month's face to face staff training with a brief video. Here's an idea from a Sticky Faith church:

"At Frontline we host quarterly trainings for all of our student ministry leaders. Over time we noticed a trend of volunteers attending less frequently. This became problematic, because it was the main place where we shared vision and important information about where we were headed as a ministry. We needed to rethink how we were training.

Our adult volunteers have their own private Facebook group for communicating information, so we decided to focus our energies there. Each week we took a 'core concept' we learned from the Sticky Faith Cohort or from books we read, recorded a five-minute video on an iPhone (think content, not quality), and uploaded it to the Facebook group. We gave each leader five days to respond back to the video with a thought or an idea about how they would implement that week's concept into their ministry.

This was helpful in a few ways:

1. Rather than only sharing vision four times per year, we were able to share it every week of the year.
2. Leaders didn't have to attend an all-day meeting, but could participate on their own time.
3. Since all of our volunteers were already on Facebook, it didn't feel like they were doing something extra.
4. They were fully engaged, because we expected them to respond once per week.
5. The videos introduced bite-sized thoughts rather than hours and hours of teaching.

After we switched to this method of training, we noticed a more engaged group of leaders speaking more frequently about the Sticky Faith concepts we were trying to implement."

MATTHEW DEPREZ
INTERGENERATIONAL PASTOR
Frontline Community Church, Grand Rapids, Michigan

AFTER WE SWITCHED TO THIS METHOD OF TRAINING, WE NOTICED A MORE ENGAGED GROUP OF LEADERS SPEAKING MORE FREQUENTLY ABOUT THE STICKY FAITH CONCEPTS WE WERE TRYING TO IMPLEMENT.

Part 2
TRAINING SESSION

STICKY FAITH OVERVIEW

 # LAUNCH TIP

"The first thing our leaders needed to understand is that there's a problem. It can be very easy to coast along thinking nothing's wrong. Once your volunteers understand the problem clearly, you can move forward toward solutions together. Our staff had to remember that we had been living in Sticky Faith ideas for a long time, but our volunteers had not."

ALAN MERCER
EXECUTIVE PASTOR
Christ Community Church Leawood Campus, Kansas City, Kansas

BIG IDEA

To introduce your entire volunteer group to Sticky Faith and its implications for your ministry context

By now you and your Launch Team have probably been conditioning for Sticky Faith for some time. You may even feel mid-marathon at this point. It's important to remember that your broader volunteer team may be a few steps—or a few miles—behind you.

Before preparing this training session, you might want to take the pulse of your team by asking a few volunteers casually, "If I asked you to explain Sticky Faith, what would you say off the top of your head?" or, "When we say 'Sticky Faith,' what does that mean to you?" You'll quickly get a sense for how much they have picked up on the basics. Either way, starting with this session is a great way to get everyone on the same course and beginning to take similar steps.

▶ INSTRUCTIONAL NOTE

YOU'LL NEED:

> » The video "Faith After High School" and a way to play it (download this video at stickyfaithlaunchkit.org)
> » White board or butcher paper and markers
> » OPTIONAL: A wrapped present
> » OPTIONAL: A large printout of Mickey Mouse's head
> » One wrinkled shirt and one freshly dry-cleaned shirt, still on the hanger and wrapped in plastic
> » OPTIONAL: Copies of your Breakthrough Plan or just the main change areas and desired outcomes (see Module 1, Part 8)

▶ ADDITIONAL RESOURCES

Some leaders have found it helpful to invite their team to read copies of *Sticky Faith Youth Worker Edition* ahead of time or during this ongoing training process. The good news is that Zondervan is partnering with us to provide discounts to leaders like you who have purchased the Sticky Faith Launch Kit. Using the code "launchkit" at churchsource.com you can get a 30 percent discount on 1-5 copies, a 40 percent discount on 6-19 copies, and a 50 percent discount on 20 or more copies of this book or the parent-focused *Sticky Faith* for your congregation.

IT'S IMPORTANT TO REMEMBER THAT YOUR BROADER VOLUNTEER TEAM MAY BE A FEW STEPS—OR A FEW MILES—BEHIND YOU.

1. THE PROBLEM

By necessity, this session will focus more heavily on the problem at hand. For most ministries that become passionate about Sticky Faith, the main problem they are trying to address is this: **Young people are walking away from faith.**

SHARE THE STATISTICS

Research shows that 40-50 percent of students from good youth groups and families will drift from God and the church after high school. That's like lining up the kids in your youth ministry and counting them off one, two, one, two. The "ones" will stick with faith and the "twos" will walk away. None of us want that to be the case for our kids.

Invite leaders to put names and faces to those statistics by thinking for a moment of one or more students who have been part of your ministry in the past who now have walked away from God and church.

Then say something such as, "In order to understand more about what helps faith stick into young adulthood, the Fuller Youth Institute studied over 500 youth group graduates for three years across the transition out of high school. Their research uncovered three main shifts needed to help young people develop a faith that sticks. We're in the midst of working through what this looks like in our own context." At this point you might want to briefly describe what you've been doing so far, and point out the Launch Team members so folks know who they can approach with ideas and concerns.

▶ **VIDEO**

Show the video "Faith After High School" here. Debrief the video with these questions:

» What stood out to you the most in this video?
» What other themes did you notice?
» What similar or different experiences do you think young people from our church experience after high school?
» What questions does this raise for you about our students and about our ministry?

2. THE VISION
CAST YOUR VISION

Briefly but clearly share your vision for how your youth ministry will impact students' long-term faith. Use a simple statement that finishes a sentence such as, "I want to be part of a church that …" or, "My hope for our students is …" At FYI, we articulate it this way: **"Our vision is to equip young people with the lifelong faith they need."** Feel free to use something like that for your context. It's certainly enough to get our team up every morning to keep doing what we do!

SHARE A STORY OF FUTURE HOPE

In the first couple of training sessions, share one or more of the best stories your Launch Team has already developed (see Module 1, Part 6). After reviewing the problem and expressing a clear vision, a good story of future hope will send a clear message to your volunteers: The content of this training is going to be incredibly important.

3. POSSIBLE SOLUTIONS
BREATHE DEEP

At this point your team may be feeling a bit overwhelmed. That's okay. Remind them that you're at the beginning of a process that will span multiple months and, in fact, might take several years to begin to implement in deep, systemic ways. Share the following points (using the tangible ideas and props if possible) as a preview for what's coming. Note that this particular "Solutions" section briefly touches on potential solutions; more solutions will emerge as you continue to work together through the training materials.

Say something like, "As the Fuller Youth Institute explored the research, three major shifts emerged that are needed in ministries like ours." Then use the ideas below to help you illustrate the three points briefly.

FROM A BEHAVIOR-BASED GOSPEL TO A GRACE-BASED GOSPEL

On a white board or butcher paper, create two lists. Title one list "Do's" and the other "Don'ts." Explain to your team that teenagers tend to understand the gospel more as a list of behaviors than an experience of God's grace. Ask your team to fill in the lists very quickly by yelling out behaviors for "Good Christians" on the two lists. Write down their answers in the appropriate columns. (You may want two writers, one for each column, in order to keep up.)

After compiling the lists, briefly explain how this kind of gospel is different from one founded in grace. If it doesn't feel too cheesy, you might even pull out a wrapped present at this point. (Bonus points if you actually wrap up a treat for each member of your team!) Remind them of the grace of the gospel, a free gift from God that is totally unearned. As we experience grace, our behaviors—our good works and our obedience to God—flow out of gratitude in response to that grace.

FROM A TWO-TABLE CHURCH TO A CHURCH THAT WELCOMES YOUNG PEOPLE AROUND ONE FAMILY TABLE

At FYI, we often talk about the two-table church, in which adults and kids are segregated into different ministries and different physical locations, much like having a "kids' table" at a family gathering. Another image to describe this is a one-eared Mickey Mouse. Draw a large circle on your white board representing Mickey's head and then draw a smaller circle for an ear on one side. In true Disney fashion, the ear should barely touch the head (you could also print out a big Mickey Mouse image to illustrate this point). Youth ministry is like this. Typically in the church we put all the adults in "big church" and siloize the kids in their own world. The two age groups touch a bit, but not much. Illustrate a few ways this is true in your own congregation.

Explain that instead of this model, you'd love to see a church where youth are folded into the life of the whole body. Youth ministry is still incredibly important, but the days of isolated youth ministry need to come to an end. Sticky Faith research shows that young people who are connected with intergenerational relationships tend to have stronger faith across the transition into adulthood.

FROM "DRY-CLEANER PARENTING" TO MINISTRY PARTNERSHIP

Bring one wrinkled shirt and one fresh-ly dry-cleaned shirt, still on the hanger and wrapped in plastic. Explain that some parents approach youth group like a dry cleaners, hoping to drop off their kids with you and pick them up again sixty or nine-ty minutes later, squeaky clean and freshly pressed. These parents have outsourced the spiritual growth of their kids to your team.

Rather than fueling this model, Sticky Faith requires a shift toward more part-nership with parents. When families know we're on their team, not just replacing them, they will often step up and engage their kids' faith more intentionally.

▶ **INSTRUCTIONAL NOTE**
KEEP IT SHORT!
Remember that this is just a drive-by tour of the main points, not an in-depth expedition. Resist the temptation to over-explain, and assure volunteers that you'll spend entire sessions together on each of these topics separately.

If your church is familiar with Orange (see whatisorange.org and the book *Think Orange* by Reggie Joiner), you know that the color can be a way to talk about partnership. Yel-low represents the church, the light of the world. Red represents the home, full of love and connection. Orange is what emerges when they come together, when the power of the family and the power of the church unite in the life of a young person. This can be a great illustration to use with your team.

---

4. PRACTICAL NEXT STEPS

What now? Again, all of this might feel like your team is drinking water from a fire hose. Depending on how much time you have, you may want to gauge volunteers' level of understanding at this point. Ask for questions or reflections that popped up as you were sharing the three main shifts Sticky Faith suggests. You may want to address some of these questions or write them down for the future.

Share your plan. This is a great time to share again about the Launch Team and reveal the main emphases of your Breakthrough Plan. Tell volunteers that this smaller team has been exploring and developing strategies for change, and over the coming months you'll be inviting them into those strategies more and more.

Watch and listen. One practical next step is for your volunteers to begin watching and listening more carefully to young people, parents, and the church as a whole. Invite them to consider:

» What evidence do you see of the problem of young people walking away from faith?
» What strengths and weaknesses do you notice about our church that either support or challenge the three main Sticky Faith shifts?
» Where do you see signs of hope that we can learn from in this process?

5. REFLECT + PRAY

Break into groups of two or three and, depending on the size of your whole group, assign the following prayer topics to one or more smaller groups for prayer. Be sure to let them know how long you're giving them and what they should do when they conclude their prayer. Feel free to narrow down these topics or include others:

» Young people who have walked away from faith and those you've lost track of

» Students preparing to transition out of high school and into the next season of life

» All of the students in your ministry—that their understanding of the gospel would be deep and that it would truly transform their lives

» Parents of students—that God would empower them to nurture faith in their kids, and that your ministry would form stronger bonds of partnership with parents

» Intergenerational relationships in your church—those that exist now, and ones yet to be forged; pray for deeper connections across age-level ministries and for creative ideas to spark new friendships between young and old

CROWDSOURCE EVEN BETTER IDEAS

We tapped into on-the-ground ministry leaders to generate ideas for these volunteer training sessions, and we think they're pretty good. But we also bet you have some stellar ideas of your own for how to help volunteers grasp Sticky Faith. On stickyfaith-launchkit.org we've created a forum where leaders can crowdsource ideas for volunteer training, parent engagement, and other aspects of Sticky Faith implementation. Join the discussion and pitch your idea or question to the community.

Part 3
TRAINING SESSION

STORIES OF FUTURE HOPE

LAUNCH TIP

"The more we communicated and told stories, the more the volunteers ended up using the same language as they talked about the youth ministry. We trained volunteers by having them read *Sticky Faith*, holding workshops, and contextualizing the findings to our congregation. My favorite moments now are when leaders connect the dots about putting Sticky Faith in action. Last night some volunteers suggested that we create an all-church teaching series because it will promote dialogue between parents and kids. Great idea!"

TIM GALLEHER
PASTOR OF YOUTH AND FAMILY MINISTRIES
Saratoga Federated Church, Saratoga, California

BIG IDEA

To help volunteers internalize your Sticky Faith vision by crafting their own stories of future hope

By now, you've spent a lot of time capturing, creating, and telling stories of future hope. You may even have noticed that these stories have personally affected you more powerfully than any other part of this launch process.

▶ **INSTRUCTIONAL NOTE**
If you're scratching your head wondering what "stories of future hope" means, loop back right now to Module 1, Part 6.

We all know that stories have power, and nothing captures our hearts and our dreams like a good story. You've had an incredible chance to internalize a vision for Sticky Faith in your congregation by engaging with these stories. This session gives your volunteers a chance to experience something similar. It's good for them to hear the stories you've captured and created, but it's even more powerful for them to capture and create their *own* stories.

▶ **INSTRUCTIONAL NOTE**

YOU'LL NEED:

» One or both of these videos and a way to play them: "Where do I find stories to introduce something new?" and "What should I do once I find a good story?" (download these videos at stickyfaithlaunchkit.org)

» OPTIONAL: Copies of one of your existing stories of future hope from Module 1, Part 6

» OPTIONAL: A copy of Dr. Martin Luther King, Jr.'s "I Have a Dream" speech, which can be found in various places online, including YouTube

» HANDOUT: "Imaginary Stories of Future Hope" (download this handout at stickyfaithlaunchkit.org)

» Pens for volunteers

1. THE PROBLEM

REVIEW THE PROBLEM

You'll have a chance to talk about the problem in each training session. It will be tempting to brush this part off or ignore it. Remember that if volunteers don't have a clear concept of the problem, they won't be able to see the importance of the solution, and they won't be able to see themselves as a part of the solution.

Given your leadership role, you're knee-deep (or maybe waist-deep, or fully swimming) in all things Sticky Faith. Your volunteers only think about it when you bring it up. They're like sunbathers on the beach who occasionally walk down to the water to dip in their toes.

That's why it's important to include a clear description of the problem in every training session. You don't need to say the same thing every week, but you do need to clearly establish the problem before you jump into the solution. Use statistics, but also contextualize the problem to your congregation and community.

TRY SOMETHING LIKE THIS:

"Research shows that 40-50 percent of students from good youth groups and families will drift from God and the church after high school. Imagine taking a picture of our students or the students in your small group. Now imagine getting out a red pen and marking through half of their faces."

IT'S GOOD FOR THEM TO HEAR THE STORIES YOU'VE CAPTURED AND CREATED, BUT IT'S EVEN MORE POWERFUL FOR THEM TO CAPTURE AND CREATE THEIR *OWN* STORIES.

2. THE VISION

TRANSITION

Transition from the Problem section with a strong statement of dissatisfaction. When we train, we tend to say something along the lines of, "As a youth worker, I'm not satisfied with 40-50 percent of our students drifting away. Are you?"

CAST YOUR VISION

Briefly but clearly repeat your vision for how your church and ministry will impact your students. Use a simple statement that finishes a sentence like, "I think students need us to be a place that ..."

SHARE A STORY OF FUTURE HOPE

In this session, share one of the best stories you already have as a Launch Team. The volunteers gathered will be writing more, but hearing your story (even if they've heard it before) is important.

▶ INSTRUCTIONAL NOTE

ABOUT REDUNDANCY AND REPETITION

After doing this several times, you'll be tempted to think you are getting redundant or you'll be worried that your volunteers have already heard the story you're sharing. Brush that temptation aside. The whole point of casting vision by sharing stories of future hope is repetition. You want your volunteers to be familiar enough with the stories to be able to share them on their own, and that takes repetition.

3. POSSIBLE SOLUTIONS

TRANSITION

Transition into the Solution section by saying something such as, "Today we're going to spend time thinking about the future of our students—not just teenagers in general, but the ones in our ministry, the ones we know and love."

STORIES OF FUTURE HOPE

Train your volunteers on the concept of stories of future hope explained in detail in Module 1, Part 6. Teach them the concept. Give them an example. Tell them why you chose the story you chose to tell in the Vision section. You may want to include one of these clips:

▶ **VIDEO**

Download the four-minute video "Where do I find stories to introduce something new?" from stickyfaithlaunchkit.org. Watch this video if you're in need of a practical example of locating Sticky Faith stories in your congregation.

▶ **VIDEO**

Here's one more video to help round out this critical topic with a story from a Sticky Faith church! Download the three-minute video "What should I do once I find a good story?" at stickyfaithlaunchkit.org.

You'll definitely want to give your volunteers a few examples. Use the Sticky Faith videos, but also feel free to look elsewhere. You can find other examples of this sort of vision casting in the news or online. Politicians use this strategy all the time—especially during campaigns—and so do major brands like Nike or Apple. If some of your volunteers are in leadership positions, they may also have great examples of this type of story from your church or other organizations.

4. PRACTICAL NEXT STEPS
TWO TYPES

There are two types of stories of future hope. The first is a true story of something that has already happened that clearly illustrates what you'd like to see more broadly. Perhaps this is a story of a former student whose faith was tested but stayed strong through college, or a story from a mission trip that captures the experience you hope all students can have on future mission trips.

The second type of story of future hope is an imaginary story about a real person that illustrates the future you'd like to see. Think of Martin Luther King Jr.'s 1963 "I Have a Dream" speech. He's describing a possible future for real people, and there is something powerful about the emotions it stirs. Instead of simply and dryly saying, "Here's a list of the things I hope this movement accomplishes," he says, "I have a dream," and the results have been legendary.

▶ VIDEO
Videos of Dr. King's speech can be found in various places online, including YouTube. Depending on how much time you have available, you may want to show a clip to your group.

I HAVE A DREAM THAT ONE DAY ON THE RED HILLS OF GEORGIA, THE SONS OF FORMER SLAVES AND THE SONS OF FORMER SLAVE OWNERS WILL BE ABLE TO SIT DOWN TOGETHER AT THE TABLE OF BROTHERHOOD.

I HAVE A DREAM THAT ONE DAY EVEN THE STATE OF MISSISSIPPI, A STATE SWELTERING WITH THE HEAT OF INJUSTICE, SWELTERING WITH THE HEAT OF OPPRESSION, WILL BE TRANSFORMED INTO AN OASIS OF FREEDOM AND JUSTICE.

I HAVE A DREAM THAT MY FOUR LITTLE CHILDREN WILL ONE DAY LIVE IN A NATION WHERE THEY WILL NOT BE JUDGED BY THE COLOR OF THEIR SKIN BUT BY THE CONTENT OF THEIR CHARACTER.

I HAVE A DREAM TODAY.

I HAVE A DREAM THAT ONE DAY, DOWN IN ALABAMA, WITH ITS VICIOUS RACISTS, WITH ITS GOVERNOR HAVING HIS LIPS DRIPPING WITH THE WORDS OF INTERPOSITION AND NULLIFICATION; ONE DAY RIGHT THERE IN ALABAMA, LITTLE BLACK BOYS AND BLACK GIRLS WILL BE ABLE TO JOIN HANDS WITH LITTLE WHITE BOYS AND WHITE GIRLS AS SISTERS AND BROTHERS.

I HAVE A DREAM TODAY.[1]

---

1   Martin Luther King, Jr., "I Have a Dream" speech, August 28, 1963, Washington, D.C.

PRACTICE
To help make this practical, create sufficient time and space for your volunteers to practice telling these two types of stories of future hope.

TRUE STORIES OF FUTURE HOPE
Break them into groups of three to five, and have each group identify one true story of future hope—a story from one of your students or families that illustrates a future they'd like to see for all students. If you have time, allow each group to share.

IMAGINARY STORIES OF FUTURE HOPE
Have every volunteer pick one current student about whom they'll do this exercise. Give them the "Imaginary Stories of Future Hope" handout and a pen, and ask them to imagine that student's life one to three years in the future. Give them ten to fifteen minutes to complete this activity.

▶ **HANDOUT**   ⟶
IMAGINARY STORIES OF FUTURE HOPE
Available to the right, as well as online.

IMAGINARY STORIES OF FUTURE HOPE

YOUR NAME:

STUDENT'S NAME:

CURRENT GRADE:

CURRENT AGE:

....

IMAGINE THIS STUDENT 1-3 YEARS FROM NOW.

1. Describe the basics of this student's life as you imagine they'll be. Where does he live? What is she doing? What is important to him?

2. Describe one imaginary scenario that this student will likely face (choosing a major, going to a party in college, comforting a friend who has experienced a tragedy, getting a job, dating, entering the military, etc.).

3. Describe how you hope the student will respond in the scenario. Connect the student's response to an experience in your ministry, the congregation, or her family as a result of your Sticky Faith dreams.

4. Put it all together and write it as a story. This is your story of future hope for this student.

HERE ARE TWO EXAMPLES OF IMAGINARY STORIES OF FUTURE HOPE FROM A STICKY FAITH COHORT CHURCH THAT DECIDED TO CONNECT THE STORIES TO ONE ANOTHER.

 STORY #1

It's April 2015. Kari is finishing up her freshman year at State University. It's her second year as a small group leader in the middle school ministry—something she started as a junior in high school after volunteering on the children's ministry team. When asked, she describes her faith as "stronger than ever—not because I know what I believe, but because I'm understanding that faith is something that's always changing and something I'm always discovering more of."

It's hard for her to point to the reasons she's still a Christian when many students at the university have more or less abandoned their faith during their first year of college. But she's able to verbalize that there have been so many people "there for her" throughout her life (parents, friends, small group leaders, and now her roommate). She knows that sharing life with her small group girls (who are now finishing seventh grade) is what she's supposed to do.

When asked about the role the youth group played in her life, she mentions three specific things: "I'm still friends with the people I met there. Even though some of them moved away, we keep in contact and I know they'll always love me. ... I remember when my small group leader from my senior year called me during midterms last semester. I was pretty overwhelmed with papers and exams, and the stress was causing a lot of people around me to do crazy things. I think if she hadn't have called me that Thursday evening, I might have gone crazy or given up on school that weekend. ... There was one program at church toward the end of our senior year where we practiced breathing. After we became aware of our breathing, we asked, 'Who am I?' and reflected on 'Who God Is' as an answer to that question. It was really calming. This year, every time I get stressed or scared, I go to the library and do that again. It helps me feel centered and reminds me of those truths."

STORY #2

It's November 2016. Mandi is talking with Kari, her small group leader of three years. She's really glad that Kari is her leader again this year, especially since she is in eighth grade now. Kari and Mandi are talking about the worship service from last Sunday. Mandi used to think that she would hate it when she got to junior high and had to go to the adult worship service every Sunday morning, but it's actually not so bad. She didn't realize that her dad would keep on talking to her about what they learned, even though they don't use the resources provided by the fifth and sixth grade ministry anymore. And now that she's older, she's glad she still feels comfortable talking to her dad about her faith, "which is weird, 'cause I don't like talking about much with him."

YOUTH MINISTRIES CAN EASILY GET BOGGED DOWN IN THE ISSUES AND PROBLEMS OF ADOLESCENCE. PART OF THE GOAL OF CREATING THESE STORIES IS TO HELP STRIKE A BALANCE BETWEEN A MINISTRY THAT IS IN TUNE WITH THE PRESENT WHILE ALSO PREPARING STUDENTS FOR THE FUTURE.

The stories your volunteers come up with don't have to be perfect. The point is for them to practice thinking about young people's futures, because everything you do now helps prepare them for their future. Youth ministries can easily get bogged down in the issues and problems of adolescence. Part of the goal of creating these stories is to help strike a balance between a ministry that is in tune with the present while also preparing students for the future.

By the end of this training, you'll have a stack of stories of future hope for your students. If you have time in the meeting, have each person share their story with someone else.

ASSIGN

If your volunteers are responsible for specific students (in a small group, etc.), give them the assignment to create a story of future hope for each student. This is the most practical next step for this session because it challenges volunteers to create a clear goal for each teenager.

▶ **INSTRUCTIONAL NOTE**
At the end of this meeting, collect and make copies of all the stories that are written. You'll need them in the next couple of training sessions. Be sure to return the originals to their authors, though, for ongoing reminders and inspiration.

5. REFLECT + PRAY
REFLECT
Give your volunteers a few minutes to reflect on their own lives:
   » How would your life be different if someone had imagined a story of future hope for you when you were an adolescent?
   » What do you sense God calling you to do in the lives of the students in our ministry?

PRAY
Create space for volunteers to conclude this training by praying for their students and their students' futures. This can be done in groups or as individuals, silently, aloud, or symbolically in some creative way (for one example, see the second Bonus Idea below).

BONUS IDEA 1:
TELLING MY OWN STORY

▶ **INSTRUCTIONAL NOTE**

YOU'LL NEED:

» Copies of the handout "Telling My Own Story"
» Pens for each volunteer

Here you are, committed to invest in teenagers. How did you get to this place? Who influenced your own faith and how did they do it?

Likely not everyone on your team was raised in church or attended youth group. That's fine. In fact, that's great. Regardless of your team's individual backgrounds, God somehow brought each person to be a youth ministry volunteer, to partner with him in writing the story of hope for your students.

Use the following handout to help leaders (yourself included!) reflect on their own faith journey and its significance for ministry today. You might give everyone five to seven minutes to complete this, or if you're using it during a retreat session or extended gathering, you could allow thirty minutes or an hour for this reflection.

▶ **HANDOUT**

TELLING MY OWN STORY

Distribute the handout "Telling My Own Story," available to the right and online at stickyfaithlaunchkit.org.

Instruct volunteers to break into groups of three or four and share a few of their answers with each other for about five minutes. Then gather everyone together and ask the group to relay any common themes they heard as they shared. Note these on a white board. Close by asking the group about the kind of stories they hope are written in students' lives. Are these stories similar to what you all have experienced, or different? Explore that for a few moments, and close in prayer.

TELLING MY OWN STORY

Take a minute to identify some key characters and events in your own story by completing the following prompts. (If you did not know Jesus during one of these life stages, you have two options. You can either skip a prompt or you can choose a time frame that makes more sense with your story. For instance, instead of talking about your faith as a child, you might describe your faith last year.)

....

The top person/people who influenced my faith as a child was:
What was special about them?

....

The top person/people who influenced my faith as a teen was:
What was special about them?

....

The biggest challenge to my faith growing up was:

....

I feel like I understood and "owned" my faith when I was about _____ years old because:

....

One 'high point' of my faith as a child/teen was:

....

Write a couple of observations about your story as you reflect back on your faith journey:

BONUS IDEA 2: PRAYING FOR STORIES OF FUTURE HOPE

 ▶ INSTRUCTIONAL NOTE
YOU'LL NEED:
  » Tables
  » Butcher paper
  » Crayons or markers

Roll butcher paper over a table (or tables, depending on the size of your group) and lay out a bunch of crayons or markers. Have your team sit around the table and invite them to pray for the future of the youth and children of your church. Instead of offering words out loud, invite them to put prayers on paper. They can be written out, single words, or images. You might want to play a prayerful song during this time of writing and drawing.

When your group has finished, allow them some time to share those prayers aloud if they want. If your church is comfortable with this tradition, you may want to symbolically lay hands on the paper, offering the hopes written on it to God.

REGARDLESS OF YOUR TEAM'S INDIVIDUAL BACKGROUNDS, GOD SOMEHOW BROUGHT EACH PERSON TO BE A YOUTH MINISTRY VOLUNTEER, TO PARTNER WITH HIM IN WRITING THE STORY OF HOPE FOR YOUR STUDENTS.

Part 4
TRAINING SESSION

THE GOSPEL

BIG IDEA

To explore the gospel so your team can live and share it in a way that helps students develop a grace-based faith

You probably picked up this Sticky Faith Launch Kit because you're hoping and working so that your students' faith will stick beyond their years in youth group. But just saying that we want faith to stick isn't good enough.

We have to ask *what kind of faith* we're hoping will stick. Key to what faith looks like in a family or congregation is the way that the gospel is understood, taught, and most importantly, how it is lived.

In order to train on this topic well, you need to educate yourself well. There have been volumes written about the gospel and lives spent debating its most important points. Start by taking a dive into your church's and denomination's understanding of the gospel. Then select a few resources that will challenge and encourage you. Below are some resources we recommend to get started. As we shared in *Sticky Faith*, many adolescents have learned a gospel that focuses on behavior, and we're convinced youth ministries need to re-emphasize a grace-centered gospel.[1]

 ▶ **ADDITIONAL RESOURCES**
HERE ARE RESOURCES THAT WE'VE FOUND EXTREMELY HELPFUL:
   » *The Divine Conspiracy* by Dallas Willard, especially chapter 2, "Gospels of Sin Management"
   » *The King Jesus Gospel* by Scot McKnight
   » *Almost Christian* by Kenda Creasy Dean

---

1   See Chapter 2, "The Sticky Gospel," in *Sticky Faith Youth Worker Edition: Practical Ideas to Nurture Long-Term Faith in Teenagers*, by Kara E. Powell, Brad M. Griffin, and Cheryl A. Crawford (Grand Rapids: Zondervan, 2011).

TO EXPLORE THE GOSPEL SO YOUR TEAM CAN LIVE AND SHARE IT IN A WAY THAT HELPS STUDENTS DEVELOP A GRACE-BASED FAITH.

▶ **INSTRUCTIONAL NOTE**

YOU'LL NEED:

- » Index cards pre-printed with statements from your student assessment in Module 1, Part 5 (you'll need one set for every small group of three or four volunteers)
- » White board or butcher paper and markers
- » OPTIONAL: The video "A Gospel That Sticks" and a way to play it (download this video at stickyfaithlaunchkit.org)
- » OPTIONAL: Copies of your Breakthrough Plan if there is a change area relevant to this theme

1. THE PROBLEM
REVIEW THE PROBLEM

By now, your volunteers are probably getting more familiar with the problem. Don't give in to the temptation to stop talking about it. Remember, your volunteers rarely think about Sticky Faith outside of your meetings, so it's important to use the training time to remind them that your collective work is situated in a specific problem. This time ask someone to articulate the problem for the group. Ask them to give a brief yet clear reminder of what problem you're trying to address with Sticky Faith. Then ask how others might add to that statement or share it differently.

2. THE VISION
TRANSITION

Transition from the Problem section with a strong statement of dissatisfaction such as, "As a youth worker, this is not acceptable to me." Since you've done this a couple of times by now, make sure that you don't lose your passion here. Let it show through!

CAST YOUR VISION

Briefly remind volunteers of your vision by sharing one or more stories of future hope. After the last training session, you should have several good stories to draw from. Sharing stories you've written is a powerful way to cast vision to your volunteers, but it will pale in comparison to sharing the stories your volunteers authored themselves!

3. POSSIBLE SOLUTIONS
TRANSITION

Transition into the Solution section with a strong statement about what you'll be discussing in this session, for example, "Today we're going to dive into our personal understanding of the gospel so that we can better live it and share it with our students."

▶ **INSTRUCTIONAL NOTE**
CAUTION: A NOTE ON SENSITIVITY
If you are like a lot of youth workers, you've engaged in conversations or read books that have challenged your views about faith and scripture. That's great—it's your job to continue deepening your understanding of the gospel. However, it's very probable that most of your volunteers have not done that. They've accepted and embraced the gospel they've been taught. It's likely they are some of the most godly people you know, but they may not actively read books on theology! If that's the case, you'll need to be sensitive to the possibility that your attempts to help volunteers deepen their understanding could seem like a pretty strong critique or questioning of faith. Move slowly and be aware of who your audience is and how they are feeling.

GOSPEL ASSESSMENT

In the assessment you conducted with your Launch Team in Module 1, Part 5, you collected information on how your students defined what it means to be a Christian. Print some key quotes from that assessment on a set of index cards. Assemble your volunteers into groups of three or four and give each group a set of the cards. Give them a few minutes to read the cards and discuss these questions: **What's right? What's missing? About which points do our students seem confused?** Have each group share what they noticed, and then discuss with the group how you and the Launch Team formulated a clear picture of how your students understand the gospel.

GOSPEL OF SIN MANAGEMENT

Dallas Willard's concept of the "gospel of sin management" is one we've found extremely helpful in assessing students' and churches' view of the gospel. Take a look at our description in *Sticky Faith Youth Worker Edition* or in Willard's *Divine Conspiracy* and teach it to your volunteers if it seems relevant to your ministry or church.

GOSPEL DISPARITY

Ahead of the meeting, take time to prepare your own working definition of the gospel, possibly collaborating with other pastors at your church or your youth ministry colleagues. Use a whiteboard or butcher paper and write a summary assessment of your students' understanding of the gospel on the far left side of the board. Then write your working definition based on your advance reflection on the right. Ask your volunteers to discuss these questions:

» What are the main differences between these two definitions?
» What do we need to do to help students discover and deepen their understanding of the gospel?

ONE WAY WE DESCRIBE THE GOSPEL TO ADULTS AND STUDENTS ALIKE IS THE 5-G MODEL. THIS IS BASED ON REFORMATION THEOLOGY BUT ADAPTED TO BEGIN WITH THE FIRST "G"—GOOD—AND TO INCLUDE THE FOURTH "G"—GOD'S PEOPLE.

GOOD
God created us good, in God's image.

GUILT
We then chose to disobey God, leaving us with the guilt of sin. All of us carry this mark and it impacts us every day.

GRACE
Through the life, death, and resurrection of Jesus, God has extended grace to us to make things right and restore us to relationship with God and one another.

GOD'S PEOPLE
As we experience grace, we are adopted into the body of Christ, embodying God's reign in the world. We join the mission of God, participating in the work of God happening through God's people.

GRATITUDE
Out of this gift of grace, we respond in gratitude toward God. This is the well out of which our obedience—those behaviors—flows. In other words, the Sticky Gospel doesn't begin with behaviors nor is it dependent on behaviors. The behaviors are like a big thank-you note we offer back to God in response to grace.

▶ **VIDEO**

Check out the 3-minute video "A Gospel that Sticks," a true story about a gospel based on grace rather than rules. It may be helpful in your conversation with your volunteers.

4. PRACTICAL NEXT STEPS

YOUR PLAN

You probably already have an idea of how you'd answer those last two questions. Share your thoughts with the group, along with any new ministry thoughts or plans you have to implement changes. If any of your change areas from your Breakthrough Plan are related to the gospel, this may be a good time to give your volunteers a copy of that part of your Breakthrough Plan. The way you'll make this practical is to invite your leaders to be part of your plan. Whether that means being willing to do small group time differently, or just using a different set of vocabulary to talk about the gospel, make sure they know what you're planning so they can support that plan.

PERSONAL NEXT STEPS

The other type of next step is personal. For a moment, put aside the fact that you and your volunteers are working to help young people develop a strong faith, and invite your volunteers to consider their own faith. What can you do as individuals and as a group to deepen your understanding of the gospel … the Good News … the best news ever? Read a book together? Read one or all of the Gospels (Matthew, Mark, Luke, or John) together? Start a discussion group? Whatever it is, invite your volunteers to take the next step in their own faith and understanding of the gospel.

5. REFLECT + PRAY

REFLECT

Give your volunteers a few minutes to reflect on the gospel. Ask them to think about the origins of their understanding of the gospel and who in their life has impacted their understanding most.

PRAY

To end this training session, pray for your volunteers. (Consider asking them to take a posture that will emphasize the prayer—standing, holding hands, kneeling, etc.) Ask God to give all of you discernment and insight. Ask for clarity and a new sense of inspiration about the good news of the gospel. Ask for the courage to live out the gospel in your daily lives and with students. If it feels appropriate, invite the group to pray one-sentence prayers, naming specific students who have a critical need to understand God's grace. Finally, thank God for the grace he has shown us in Jesus.

BONUS IDEA: GOD IS NOT SANTA

 ▶ **INSTRUCTIONAL NOTE**
YOU'LL NEED:

» A copy of a clip from the movie *Elf* (see below) and a way to play it

In some ways, students see God like Santa. Santa is good, of course. Santa gives you good things on Christmas. And Santa is omniscient, just like God.[2]

But there are other ways students see God like Santa. Distribute the lyrics to the song "Santa Claus is Coming to Town," perhaps singing it together. Or play this clip from the movie *Elf*, and then discuss it with your team.

 ▶ **VIDEO**
Find the clip "Santa Claus is Coming to Town" from the 2003 movie *Elf*. You can get a copy of the DVD or search YouTube for samples. (Disclaimer: be sure to clarify the permission needed in your particular context for showing movie clips from copyrighted films.)

---

2   For a theological exploration of this idea of God and Santa, see Miroslav Volf, *Free of Charge: Giving and Forgiving in a Culture Stripped of Grace*, especially pages 26-28.

Discuss the song—and these specific lyrics—for a few moments with your team. "He sees you when you're sleeping, he knows when you're awake. He knows if you've been bad or good, so be good for goodness' sake."[3]

In a nutshell, that is the way many kids and teenagers see God. He's very much like Santa. God sees you all the time. He knows all about you. And most of all, he knows if you are good or bad, and he wants you to be good. And when you try to be good, it's for goodness' sake, not for Christ's sake or the kingdom's sake.

Santa cares most about your behaviors—how well you keep to the do's and don'ts—so that you can stay on the nice list and off the naughty list. Santa's goodness to you is contingent on your actions. And Santa's 'gospel' is about moralism—it's nice to be nice and it's good to be good.

That's not really "good news" at all, is it? One of our goals, then, is to remind young people (and one another) that God is not Santa.

> SANTA'S 'GOSPEL' IS ABOUT MORALISM— IT'S NICE TO BE NICE AND IT'S GOOD TO BE GOOD.
>
> THAT'S NOT REALLY "GOOD NEWS" AT ALL, IS IT? ONE OF OUR GOALS, THEN, IS TO REMIND YOUNG PEOPLE (AND ONE ANOTHER) THAT GOD IS NOT SANTA.

---

3   John Frederick Coots and Haven Gillespie, "Santa Claus Is Coming to Town," 1934.

Part 5
TRAINING SESSION

ENGAGING FAMILIES

BIG IDEA

To understand the importance of parents in teenagers' faith, and then to work to strengthen your partnership with parents

According to sociologist Christian Smith, "Most teenagers and their parents may not realize it, but a lot of research in the sociology of religion suggests that the most important social influence in shaping young people's religious lives is the religious life modeled and taught to them by their parents."[1] Or as we heard Smith say on a panel discussion here at Fuller, "When it comes to kids' faith, parents get what they are."[2] The point is that parents tend to play the most influential roles in the spiritual lives of their kids.

 ## LAUNCH TIP

If you haven't yet read the work of the National Study of Youth and Religion, you may find it helpful (http://www.youthandreligion.org/). We especially recommend the books *Soul Searching* (Christian Smith and Melina Lundquist Denton), *Souls in Transition* (Christian Smith and Patricia Snell), and *Almost Christian* (Kenda Creasy Dean) for a deeper look at this nationwide study.

 ▶ **INSTRUCTIONAL NOTE**
YOU'LL NEED:

- » White board or butcher paper and markers
- » The video "Dry-Cleaner Parents" and a way to play it (download this video at stickyfaithlaunchkit.org)
- » Index cards and pens for volunteers
- » OPTIONAL: Copies of your Breakthrough Plan if there is a change area relevant to this theme

---

1   Christian Smith with Melinda Lundquist Denton, *Soul Searching: The Religious and Spiritual Lives of American Teenagers* (Oxford University Press, 2009), 56.

2   Listen to the "Soul Searching" panel discussion from March 2008 at the FYI website: http://fulleryouthinstitute.org/podcast/soul-searching-panel.

1. THE PROBLEM

Your volunteers have heard your reiteration of the problem. Now it's their turn to describe the problem. Divide them into groups of two or three and have them articulate the big-picture problem to one another as if they were having a conversation in the church hallway with another adult. Afterward, have each group share how that conversation went. What do they wish they were better able to put into words? Take notes on that for future training sessions or email follow up with your team.

2. THE VISION

STORIES OF FUTURE HOPE

Share another story of future hope written by a volunteer in a prior training session (if you're skipping around, see Module 2, Part 3). Afterward, ask the group: "How does this story capture our vision for Sticky Faith?"

3. POSSIBLE SOLUTIONS

TRANSITION

Transition into the Solution section by saying something such as, "We're going to spend today's session exploring how we can best interact with and support parents in our ministry."

THE IMPORTANCE OF PARENTS

Take several minutes to share about the importance of parents in the lives of adolescents. Use the quotes from Christian Smith above in the Big Idea of this session, or any other helpful parts from Module 3 (which is all about parents), to help illustrate the point. It probably won't take long for you to convince your volunteers of the importance of parents; they've already witnessed it in both positive and negative ways.

▶ VIDEO

Download the four-minute video "Dry-Cleaner Parents" from stickyfaithlaunchkit.org to show your team.

DRY-CLEANER PARENTS

Show the video "Dry-Cleaner Parents," and then have groups of three to five discuss the advice Kara gives in the video:

» Start early.
» Take baby steps.
» Become a student of parents.

Ask groups to discuss whether they agree or disagree and what else they might add. Did the metaphor of a dry cleaner make sense? Call on a few groups to share their thoughts. Make sure to ask those volunteers who are parents to share their reactions from a parent perspective.

ENABLING

Take a minute as a group to discuss ways your ministry enables parents to be dry-cleaner families. Make sure to write down everything that volunteers suggest; there might be something you haven't thought of yet. Plus, when you have a chance to talk to parents, it might help you to be able to point to a list created by volunteers.

BRAINSTORM BABY STEPS

Using a whiteboard or butcher paper, create a list of baby steps you can take toward partnering with parents as a ministry, both as a whole team and as individual volunteers. Consider using three columns—first steps, second steps, and third steps—and place each idea in the column where you think it belongs. Since the comfort level of your volunteers will span a wide range on this topic, the columns will allow people of all comfort levels to see what a next step could look like for them.

STORIES

If there are one or two volunteers who have developed great relationships with parents, ask them in advance if they would share during this training how those relationships developed and what they've done to support them. This will inspire other volunteers to take the first step.

4. PRACTICAL NEXT STEPS

Divide into groups of two or three. Ask volunteers to choose one thing from the brainstorming list that they can do to support parents and increase their connection with them. If it didn't make the list, make sure to add Kara's nine-word suggestion from the video: "How can I pray for you and your family?"

TAKE ACTION

Ask your volunteers to write down their next step on two index cards. They will take home one of the cards and will give the other to you. Tell them you are going to pray for each of them and for these action steps in the coming weeks. If you have capacity to do so (based on the size of your team), also follow up with volunteers individually in about a month to see how it's going and what they're learning as they take these steps with parents.

YOUR PLAN

If you have a specific ministry change area or initiative related to this area as part of your Breakthrough Plan, share that with your volunteers during this training.

5. REFLECT + PRAY
REFLECT

Give your volunteers three to five minutes and ask them to think about the relationships their students have with their parents. Are they strained? positive? negative? nonexistent?

PRAY

In groups of two or three, ask your volunteers to pray for parents. Encourage them to pray specifically by name and situation.

PARENTS TEND TO PLAY THE MOST INFLUENTIAL ROLES IN THE SPIRITUAL LIVES OF THEIR KIDS.

BONUS IDEA 1: CLEAN AND PRESSED

 ▶ **INSTRUCTIONAL NOTE**

YOU'LL NEED:

» Butcher paper

» Tape

» Markers or crayons

Before your session, draw an outline of a teenager on butcher paper and cut it out. Tape your paper student to the wall. Give him or her a name. Then gather up some markers or crayons and welcome your volunteer team.

Explain to volunteers that some parents have a dry-cleaner mentality when it comes to our youth ministry. They want to drop off their kids with us all dirty and wrinkled, and then pick them up sixty or ninety minutes later cleaned and pressed. In many ways, this is our fault. Often we have not partnered with families as well as we could have partnered. Rather than just criticize "those parents," you're going to take a few minutes to understand this better.

Next ask your volunteers to identify the "dirt" and "wrinkles" that parents see in their kids—the concerns they have about their behavior, as well as their concerns about spiritual development. Note that many of these are very legitimate concerns. These are also the areas where parents expect your ministry to step in and "clean" and "press." Invite volunteers to come up and write those concerns on the paper teenager. Afterward, read them out to the group.

Note that obviously we cannot iron out these things by seeing students once or even twice a week. These are complex and challenging realities. Many of parents' concerns include issues far beyond our realm of influence. And when it comes down to it, God is the one who does any changing or "cleaning," not us.

What we *can* do is recognize the stress and fear many parents experience, and we can think about what it might look like to join their support team.

Instruct volunteers to pair up and role-play a conversation in which one person is the youth leader and the other is a parent. The parent raises an issue about his or her child with the expectation that the youth leader will take the lead in "fixing" the problem. The youth leader's role in the conversation is to practice modeling partnership instead of dry cleaning. Afterward, debrief with the group what you learned from those conversations.

BONUS IDEA 2:
GETTING ON A PARENT'S TEAM

 ▶ INSTRUCTIONAL NOTE

THIS EXERCISE WILL TAKE A BIT MORE PREPARATION. YOU'LL NEED:

» Before your meeting, assemble an "in their shoes" visual kit for your volunteers.
» Ask a parent for some items that represent himself and his relationship with his child, such as photographs, outfits from when his child was younger, a well-loved Bible or book they read together, or an object that represents a favorite activity they do together.
» Also be sure to get a pair of the parent's shoes.

Set up the visual on a table in the center of your meeting, and say something like the following to your volunteer team: "As a volunteer (and for me as a youth pastor!) it's easy to think that our focus should be entirely on students. But we serve students best when we also connect with their families. For a few minutes, I want us to slip out of our own shoes and put on someone else's: a parent's. If you are a parent, then you will try to imagine another family in addition to your own. If you're not, just focus on wearing a parent's shoes for a few moments."

Give your team a few minutes to look at the items in the parental visual kit silently. Then ask these reflection questions:

» What do you notice about these items? What stands out to you?
» Taking the perspective of a parent of a student in our youth group, what are you hoping for your child?
» What are you afraid of in your child's life?
» What might you worry about when it comes to youth group, even if you want to be supportive?
» What are you hoping for from our youth ministry? What do you hope we will do for your kid?
» What would "partnership" look like to you on a weekly basis?

Close by praying together for all of those who wear "parent shoes" in your congregation. Be sure to also pray for those who are raising kids, such as foster parents, aunts and uncles, or grandparents. Pray for the parents you never see. Pray that God would stir your team to build stronger bonds of partnership with families of all kinds in your ministry.

Part 6
TRAINING SESSION

INTER-GENERATIONAL MINISTRY

▶ **INSTRUCTIONAL NOTE**

This training session is directly connected to Module 4, "Taking Sticky Faith to the Whole Church." You may want to read that module before leading this session, in particular Part 3: "Tips, Tools, and Experiments in Intergenerational Ministry."

BIG IDEA

To inspire volunteers to be advocates for intergenerational relationships in your church

While there's no "silver bullet" for Sticky Faith, the one finding in our research that comes closest is boosting intergenerational connections. We found that high school and college students who experience more intergenerational worship and relationships tend to have higher faith maturity. Beyond that, contact with at least one adult from the congregation outside the youth ministry during college is linked with Sticky Faith.

Unfortunately, when we asked high school seniors to rank sources of support in their church, adults in the congregation ranked last by far. In many congregations, intergenerational relationships tend to be weak or mostly nonexistent.

▶ **INSTRUCTIONAL NOTE**

YOU'LL NEED:
- » White board or butcher paper and markers
- » The video "A Tale of Two Tables" and a way to play it (download this video at stickyfaithlaunchkit.org)
- » OPTIONAL: The video "Jonah & Bob: A Sticky Faith Story" and a way to play it (download this video at stickyfaithlaunchkit.org)
- » OPTIONAL: Copies of your Breakthrough Plan if there is a change area relevant to this theme
- » Paper and pens for volunteers

1. THE PROBLEM

The big problem of young people walking away from faith is tied to the problem of generational segregation in churches. We often describe this as something like the "adult table" and "kids' table" at big family gatherings—two tables, two very different experiences.

▶ VIDEO

You may want to start this section by showing the one and a half minute video "A Tale of Two Tables" about intergenerational churches (download at stickyfaithlaunchkit.org). After the video, ask your volunteers to discuss these questions in groups of three to five:

» What is your initial reaction to this video and the metaphor of the "kids' table"?

» Do you think this describes our church? To what degree?

While young people need to be on their own sometimes, in our churches we have often defaulted to separating generations almost exclusively. It will help to think of a clear example or story from your church that sets this problem up well. For example, one congregation realized that children and teenagers never shared Communion with the congregation because they were always in age-level ministries. This exclusion from the Communion table became emblematic of the vast age segregation across their ministries.

2. THE VISION

You've shared your Sticky Faith vision over and over. Ask volunteers to connect this vision with bringing the generations together around young people. What would it look like to create shared-table experiences in your congregation? Perhaps there is a Story of Future Hope written by one of your volunteers that highlights intergenerational relationships. If so, ask them to share it.

3. POSSIBLE SOLUTIONS
FINDINGS

Share the Sticky Faith findings about intergenerational churches mentioned above in the Big Idea.[1] Wonder aloud what young people in your church experience when it comes to intergenerational worship, relationships, and contact after high school.

5:1

One of the hallmarks of Sticky Faith has been reversing the 5:1 ratio in ministry. What would it look like for your team to advocate for every young person in your church to have five adults in their lives that help support and care for them?

Your volunteers are a huge, irreplaceable part of this equation (certainly the people in the room represent one of the five for multiple students), but we think students need more than the total of your ministry team. Share this with your volunteers in a way that encourages them to lean into their role but also inspires them to be advocates for their students among the congregation. They may be strategically positioned to connect students with adult friends, family, and colleagues who may be able to play an important support role.

▶ VIDEO

It might be helpful to show the two-minute video "Jonah & Bob: A Sticky Faith Story" about an informal relationship that developed between a teenager and an older adult (download at stickyfaithlaunchkit.org).

After the video, ask your volunteers to discuss these questions in groups of three to five:

» What encourages you about this story?
» How is this relationship connected to Sticky Faith?
» Can you think of an example of a "Jonah and Bob" in our congregation?
» What ideas does this spark for other relationships like this that could develop in our congregation?

For example, if one of your volunteers knows that a student needs some help on a physics project, they may introduce the student to their friend who is an engineer. Or perhaps a volunteer knows a businessperson who would meet with a student interested in a career in business. The connections are endless, and this is your chance to encourage volunteers that they can be important links in each student's 5:1 web of relationships. This is another great place to share a story of future hope that applies—if there are instances of this already happening, make sure everyone knows!

▶ **INSTRUCTIONAL NOTE**
DON'T FORGET THE PARENTS!
Linking back to the previous training session on parents, this is a good spot to ask your volunteers how the 5:1 strategy relates to partnering with families. Ideally, parents are equipped to create the 5:1 web of relationships for their kids and our role is to support and enhance their work. But of course this isn't going to be true of every family. What would it look like for your team to inspire parents to take next steps in sparking 5:1 relationships and to empower them to do so?

CHURCH CULTURE + YOUR PLAN
If your church has a culture that keeps young people mostly separate from older people, your volunteers will be key players in helping to change the culture. They are, after all, part of the adult population in your church. Helping them see age segregation as a problem is the first step. You may have a specific way you'd like them to help further goals in your Breakthrough Plan.

4. PRACTICAL NEXT STEPS

Below are two next steps related to advocacy. You may want to focus on just one or on both, depending on your volunteers and your assessment of your church's culture.

1. ADVOCACY FOR 5:1

Create space for your volunteers to think through specific students in your ministry. Have them answer these questions and write down their plans:

» Who in our church has a similar interest as this student?

» What would be the best way to introduce the student (and their parents) and this person to each other?

2. ADVOCACY FOR CULTURAL CHANGE

As we mentioned, if changing your church's culture is a part of your Breakthrough Plan, you'll definitely want to share that with your volunteers and give them specific ways they can help you accomplish the plan. But more generally, you may want to ask them to be advocates for cultural change. They can do this in at least two ways:

» Through the personal conversations they have with other church members. Ask them to help others see the value of strengthening intergenerational community. Most likely, your volunteers would say that their relationships with young people have been just as transformative for them as they have been for the young people. If that is the case, help them articulate it in a way that they can share with other adults. This is an important way your volunteers can help adults see that all the generations need one another.

» Ask them to encourage their students to participate in church-wide activities with an open attitude. If your church has a strong culture of separation, chances are good that your students don't feel welcome or needed in church-wide services and activities. Your team can help them see that they are needed and welcome, and that they should see themselves as part of the church, not just part of the youth ministry. You might even choose an upcoming church-wide activity to attend as a small group.

Ask volunteers to discuss how they can advocate in one of these two ways. Ask them to choose one advocacy method and then write two action steps for what they will do in the next month. Here are some example action steps:

» Invite a student to participate in a Bible study, prayer meeting, or Sunday school class that is typically only attended by adults.

» Invite a student to help serve in the nursery, on the tech team, or with the weekly food outreach.

» Tell a fellow church member a story about how being part of students' lives has transformed you or taught you something you did not know about God.

5. REFLECT + PRAY

End this session by leading a directed prayer. Say each of the prompts below out loud, and give your volunteers one or two minutes between each prompt to pray aloud as a whole group or in groups of two.

» Pray for the adults in our church.

» Pray for the young people in our church.

» Pray for unity in our church.

» Ask God to give both the adults and the young people an openness to get to know each other.

» Pray for a specific student who needs another adult in his or her life. Ask God to provide someone from our church community.

IF YOUR CHURCH
HAS A CULTURE
THAT KEEPS YOUNG
PEOPLE MOSTLY
SEPARATE FROM
OLDER PEOPLE, YOUR
VOLUNTEERS WILL
BE KEY PLAYERS IN
HELPING TO CHANGE
THE CULTURE.

BONUS IDEA 1: CALENDAR OF EVENTS

 ▶ **INSTRUCTIONAL NOTE**

YOU'LL NEED:

» Copies of your church's calendar of events
» Possibly copies of your youth ministry calendar of events

Distribute copies of your church's calendar of events and ask volunteers to look through the year for a few moments. Then reflect:

» What events in our church life represent potential for quality student/adult interaction?
» In what ways might one or two of these events be modified so that they are more appealing and more welcoming for teenagers?

Similarly, you could distribute your youth ministry's calendar and ask:

» Which of these events will likely already have strong adult/kid interaction?
» Which two events have the greatest potential for such interaction? What changes need to be made to these events to facilitate more interaction?

Alternatively, you might divide your team in half and have one group discuss your church's calendar and the other your youth ministry's calendar. When those discussions conclude, regroup and have each group share their thoughts.

BONUS IDEA 2: INVITE THE "OLD FOLKS"

It's likely that your volunteer leaders have a variety of experiences when it comes to intergenerational worship and relationships. Some may have grown up surrounded by people of all ages in church. Others may not have known many older Christians. Further, depending on the age span of your volunteer team, there may be one or more generations without any representation in the room when you gather.

For this exercise, invite some people who are older than your team members to join you for the last fifteen to thirty minutes of your session. These will need to be adults you have prepared ahead of time by framing the problem of generational segregation and setting forth the vision for more connection.

Ask those older adults to pray for your leaders, not only in their service role at church, but also personally. You could set up this prayer time in several ways, depending on the personality of your group. Some ideas include:

» Matching each youth leader up one on one
» Breaking into small groups of two or three volunteers with a pair of older adults
» Having just one or two guests come and pray aloud over your whole group

However you structure it, you can give your team the opportunity to be blessed by older Christians, which can serve as a snapshot of what teenagers in the youth group can experience as intergenerational relationships are strengthened. Be sure to have refreshments on hand and build in some informal time of connecting afterward.

Part 7
TRAINING SESSION

TRANSITIONS

BIG IDEA

To help your volunteers embrace the unique role they can play in students' faith development during seasons of transition

Adolescence can seem like a never-ending series of changes and transitions. Young people are changing all over. Their bodies are changing. Their brains are changing. Their ability to regulate emotions, make decisions, understand abstract ideas, imagine the future, and to think outside themselves are all changing. On top of that, their social relationships are constantly in flux. Their sense of belonging ebbs and flows. Their understanding of identity grows, shrinks, deconstructs, and reconstructs seemingly overnight.

Besides the constant change, some of life's biggest *transitions* take place in adolescence. Leaving behind childhood, receiving a driver's license, going on first dates, entering high school, and graduating high school all represent major milestones. And let's not forget to mention just surviving middle school.

In the midst of all of this change and transition, your ministry plays a unique role in walking with young people on their journey of faith.

▶ INSTRUCTIONAL NOTE

YOU'LL NEED:

» OPTIONAL: To contact a graduate (or graduates) ahead of time to help illustrate The Problem (see section 1)

» Paper and pens for volunteers

» White board or butcher paper and markers

» Copies of the "Transitions" handout (download this handout at sticky-faithlaunchkit.org)

» OPTIONAL: Copies of your Breakthrough Plan if there is a change area relevant to this theme

1. THE PROBLEM

In our Sticky Faith research, we learned that six out of seven students didn't feel prepared for the faith transition the first year after high school. What's more, young people's main advice to youth leaders three years out of high school was, "Prepare us better." Our high school graduates feel the effect of weak preparation for this transition, and they continue to feel it for several years.

In order to set up the problem for this session, you may want to contact a youth group graduate (or several) ahead of time to get their own perspective on the transition out of high school. You could do this one of several ways: by inviting graduates to respond by email with feedback on the transition; by inviting one or more to join you in person if that's feasible; or by inviting one or more to join you using an online video conferencing service. Send them several questions ahead of time exploring what the transition was like and in what ways they wish they had been better prepared.

2. THE VISION

Tell your most compelling story of future hope, even if this is the umpteenth time they've heard it. Better yet, ask one of your volunteers to share the story.

3. POSSIBLE SOLUTIONS
SET THE STAGE

Divide the volunteers into groups of three to five and distribute paper and pens. Have each group make a list of all the changes and transitions that happen in a person's life between the ages of ten and eighteen. Then list all of these on a whiteboard.

Make it more fun by adding some competition. Score the game "Boggle" style, so that points are awarded only when a group lists a change or transition that no other group listed.

DISCUSS

Take a few moments to debrief this list as a group. Ask the following questions:

» What do students need that cuts across many (and perhaps most) of these transitions?

» As you think about some of the specific transitions we've listed, what are the unique needs of a student experiencing that upheaval? For instance, a student who's moving to a new school has a unique need to make new friends.

» Regardless of the exact nature of the transition, how do you think transitions can be tools that build students' faith instead of jeopardize it?

YOU AND NO ONE ELSE

Transition to the idea that in the midst of all of these transitions, students need unconditional presence and love. Volunteers are uniquely positioned to offer this kind of presence.

Set this up by explaining that most adolescents have several significant adults in their lives: parents, teachers, coaches, extended family, and so on (hopefully at least 5, right?). But not all teenagers have someone in their life who is a *volunteer.*

From the perspective of a young person, what do parents, teachers, and most other adults have in common? Obligation. Duty. Ask a teenager why their parents love them or why their teachers care about their education, and although you'll probably hear about genuine love and care, you'll also hear "because they have to" or "because it's their job."

Ask teenagers why the volunteers in your ministry spend their time with them, and you'll get a blank stare. Volunteers play a role that almost no other adults play in young people's lives (including you, if this is your paid job): an unconditional role. **Volunteers *choose* to spend their time and energy with teenagers. They have no obligation to do so, and they get no wage for their sacrifice.**

LAUNCH TIP

Several good resources exist to help volunteers build unconditional relationships with young people. We specifically recommend chapter 13, "What Do Midadolescents Need?" of Chap Clark's book *Hurt 2.0* or chapter 6, "What Then Shall We Do" of Andy Root's book *Revisiting Relational Youth Ministry.*

4. PRACTICAL NEXT STEPS

Divide your team into groups based on specific transitions that have been mentioned so far. Let them self-select based on interest. For example, if a volunteer wants to talk about the transition to ninth grade, they mention that and see if anyone wants to join them. The huddles then focus on that specific transition, discussing the following handout:

▶ HANDOUT
TRANSITIONS
Available to the right and online at stickyfaithlaunchkit.org.

After an appropriate amount of time, invite volunteers to stay in their huddles but turn their attention to a large group discussion. Ask each subgroup to share one or two particular insights or ideas that emerged in their conversation.

Your plan. If you have a specific ministry change area or initiative related to transitions as part of your Breakthrough Plan, share that with your volunteers during this part of the training and get their input as appropriate.

▶ INSTRUCTIONAL NOTE
CREATING MILESTONES
For a boatload of ideas on how to create faith milestones for transitions across the span of childhood and adolescence, see Module 3, Part 5.

TRANSITIONS

What are the most poignant needs of a student in this particular transition? (Some of these may have been mentioned already; it's okay to repeat what's been said.)

How could you communicate your unconditional support and care for a student in the midst of this transition?

How do you think that support would make a difference in their faith?

What conversation topics would you want to address with a student who was navigating this transition?

What ideas do you have for our ministry as a whole to better support students through this particular transition?

5. REFLECT + PRAY

REFLECT

Lead your team through this exercise by asking the following prompts and giving them a minute to write their answers on paper you provide. Start by asking them to think of a particular student going through (or heading into) the transition their subgroup just discussed:

» Which student do I want to support in the midst of this transition?

» How can I let them know of my unconditional love and support for them?

» If I had the chance to talk with this student, what questions would I want to ask to help them navigate this transition? How could I help them see it as something that could build their faith?

» What would I want them to know about God in the midst of this transition?

PRAY

Now invite volunteers to turn back to their huddles and pray aloud for these students.

Close by praying aloud for your volunteers, asking God to help them see the importance of their role in the lives of teenagers. Ask God to give them the courage, energy, and perseverance they need to play their unique role.

SAYING THANKS

Take this opportunity to thank your volunteers for all they give to students on a week-to-week basis.

TAKE THIS OPPORTUNITY TO THANK YOUR VOLUNTEERS FOR ALL THEY GIVE TO STUDENTS ON A WEEK-TO-WEEK BASIS.

BONUS IDEA: CREATE A SUMMER TRANSITION EVENT

If you don't already have a way to formally acknowledge and celebrate students during their transition into significant grades, utilize this time with your team to develop some ideas. You might specifically think about programming for incoming sixth graders and incoming ninth graders. We've also heard of churches that think about incoming sixth graders, eighth graders, and twelfth graders as they are moving to the top of the "food chain" in their respective systems (depending on how your school district works). Spending time with these students in the summer before the academic year could allow them to prepare and set goals for the next season. Brainstorm with your team about an event, a brief small group series, or an element of your worship gathering that can encourage your students heading into transition years.

 ▶ **ADDITIONAL RESOURCES**

THE STICKY FAITH TEEN CURRICULUM

The *Sticky Faith Teen Curriculum* was designed to be used with high school juniors and seniors as they prepare to transition into college and adulthood. Consider gathering seniors for a monthly meeting or special weekend retreat to tackle some of these issues. Thanks to our partnership with Zondervan publishing, you can purchase a copy of the curriculum at a 30 percent discount using the code "launchkit" at churchsource.com or by calling 1-800-727-3480.

LAUNCH TIP

"One of the key lessons we learned in recruiting and training volunteers was not to under-sell the vision of what it means to be part of a Sticky Faith *movement*. As we began to cast the vision of long-term intentional discipling relationships, we found that our volunteers caught on quickly. What surprised us was how after just a short time of working with students under this vision, they were already convinced of the value of discipleship over time. This long-scope perspective has been a real sticking point for our volunteers. We have learned that asking people to commit to be a small group leader from seventh grade through graduation and beyond is not overwhelming. In fact, it provides a sense of stability as well as 'reverse mentoring,' where students impact leaders' faith growth. This has been an unexpected blessing of implementing Sticky Faith."

NATE ROSKAM
COMMUNITY LIFE PASTOR
Nampa First Nazarene, Nampa, Idaho

MODULE 03

ENGAGING PARENTS

Part 1

WHY ENGAGE PARENTS?

 LAUNCH TIP

"I wish I would've realized the power of *one*. I'll never forget sitting in Linda's kitchen. She had made a delicious lunch to share, and she wanted to know how we were *really* changing the youth ministry. She was anxious about how it affected her kids. She wanted to see how it fit her paradigm for youth ministry. As I drove to Linda's house for lunch that day, I remember thinking that I didn't have time for this one-on-one meeting. I wished she would just come to my parent meetings, read my emails, and follow up on the suggested resources we give parents.

But I walked away from that lunch date convicted that this one conversation would likely yield way more fruit than *my* generic parent meeting with my agenda and talking points. She asked her questions, shared her heart, listened, and, finally, volunteered her support. Linda became an advocate and a storyteller of our new direction because she personalized and contextualized my vision to become *our* vision. I've realized over the years that it's often the power of one person, and sometimes even one conversation, that changes things."

APRIL DIAZ
PASTOR OF HUMAN DEVELOPMENT
Newsong Church, Irvine, California

If you're a youth worker, you've probably heard the news by now: Parents trump you.[1] A growing body of research suggests that, in general, parents are the primary spiritual influences in their kids' lives.

While informative, this research is also challenging as it calls youth workers to think innovatively and systemically about their ministry approaches. So once you've created a Sticky Faith Breakthrough Plan for your ministry (see Module 1, Part 8) your excitement grows as you make plans to gain parents' support and partnership.

---

[1]   Sticky Faith collaborator Steven Argue originally wrote Part 1 of this module as an article for the Fuller Youth Institute E-Journal entitled "Getting Parents On Board (Hint: They already are): Reimagining the parent–youth worker relationship as a way forward," published May 2013. It has been modified in this version.

THE DISAPPOINTING FIRST STEPS

You envision the parents in your ministry cheering at the new ideas, thanking you for being such a thoughtful leader, and praising you for saving their children, their families, and probably their very lives.

> # AND THEN YOU HAVE THAT FIRST CONVERSATION, THAT FIRST MEETING, THAT FIRST PROGRAM CHANGE.

And nothing happens.

Blank stares.

A poorly attended "vision" meeting.

A sparse response to that email manifesto.

More questions about camp dates than your year-long formational teaching plan.

Given your disappointment, you're left scratching your head and wondering: *How do we get parents on board?*

THE WRONG QUESTION

This can be a fair question that often comes from youth workers' deep desire to support young people the best we can. It comes out of admitting that we can't do this alone, and that in itself is the sign of a more mature way of looking at youth ministry.

However, it's the wrong question for at least three reasons.

OUR VIEW OF THE RELATIONSHIP IS PROBLEMATIC
It's the wrong question because it is laced with assumptions. We should always use caution about "getting" parents or anyone to "do" anything as it creates an odd relationship between parent and youth worker. It is a symptom of a deeper, systemic problem where we assume we must "get" students, volunteers, and parents to do what we ask. Youth ministry cannot be a machine where we "get" working parts in order. It is a dynamic organism that is held together through relationships grounded in love more than programs.

OUR RESPONSE TO LITTLE BUY-IN DEFAULTS TO JUDGMENT
Just because parents aren't buying into your vision (no matter how brilliant) doesn't mean they haven't bought into loving their kids, seeking God, or wanting their family to follow Jesus. There's an unhealthy subtext we often hear among youth workers that assumes parents don't care, have been hypnotized by secularism, or are more interested in their careers than their kids. The Scriptures call this "judging." Judging occurs when we critique the heart or the motives of another person. It's one thing to call out a person on their behaviors. It's quite another thing to accuse others about their character and assumed motivations. What if we were to start with the assumption that all of us want the best for each other? Likely we'd have a better chance of starting as friends than opponents.

OUR ASSUMPTIONS START WITH PARENTS NOT CARING
The solution to "getting parents on board" is skewed if we think that parents don't care. Parents care more than many youth workers think they do. Let's therefore start with this basic assumption: Parents typically love their kids. Let's take it further: Parents love their kids more than youth leaders love their kids. If this is the case, parents are already on board and *this should be our starting place*. If we start here, our relationship with parents can be transformed.

THIS PROCESS CAN BE BEAUTIFUL, VAGUE, INSPIRING, AND CHALLENGING ALL AT THE SAME TIME.

FINDING ALTERNATIVES

It's likely that parents in your context are asking all kinds of questions about how to raise their children in the Christian faith. Some questions are thoughtful, others come out of desperation, and still others stress that they want a different faith experience for their children than they had growing up. This process can be beautiful, vague, inspiring, and challenging all at the same time.

We've come to view parents' questions in three basic categories. These categories are by no means an attempt to reduce or simplify the unique and complex needs of each of the families in your context. **Take time to listen to parents in your ministry, letting their unique questions inform the ways you engage families.**

▶ **INSTRUCTIONAL NOTE**

For more ideas on listening before leading (and some practical tools), jump back to Module 1, Parts 5-7.

Here are three common needs youth workers have heard from parents that this Launch Kit helps you address:

 HELP ME GET INFORMATION AND HAVE ACCESS TO RESOURCES WHEN I NEED THEM

Maybe it's just us, but the parent classes and seminars we offer are rarely busting at the seams. We could assume that parents aren't "on board." But likely, the reasons are more diverse. Some parents feel too overwhelmed or even ashamed. For others, the thought of a seminar answering the complex issues they are trying to navigate seems trite. Sometimes (let's be honest) our meetings aren't worth parents' investment.

We do see value in parent training meetings, and actually Part 3 of this module outlines a parent seminar you might find useful. But not all parents will respond to this approach.

Many leaders are discovering that some of our best opportunities with parents occur when we catch parents in transitional times and when we offer resources parents can access when they need them most (which almost never fits neatly into our ministry calendar).

YOU MIGHT FIND WAYS TO MEET THIS NEED BY:
- » Developing regular, informative emails to parents (updates, articles, resources). See Part 2 of this module for a fourteen-week kick-start to this idea.
- » Creating resources parents can access online (books, articles, trainings) or finding resources that already exist and pointing parents to them.
- » Offering training or connection during the times when their children are in ministry programming and parents are already on the church campus.
- » Creating touch-point experiences for parents connected with major life transitions like entering middle or high school, graduation, and other milestones. Depending on how your church practices baptism and/or some form of "confirmation" process, look for ways to tap into these faith milestones as opportunities for deeper parent engagement. See Part 5 of this module for lots of additional ideas on creating faith milestones.

HELP ME SERVE/PARTICIPATE WITH MY CHILD IN SOMETHING THAT HELPS US LIVE THE GOSPEL TOGETHER

Many parents want to do formational activities with their kids. Some don't quite know how to go about that. A shared discipleship experience creates opportunities for parents to approach an otherwise abstract and anxious topic like spirituality in a hands-on way. It creates a context for cultivating a common faith language where it hasn't yet existed in that family.

LOOK FOR OPPORTUNITIES TO CREATE THESE SHARED SPACES BY:

» Leveraging current experiences from your children's ministry and student ministry where parents and kids might interact. For example, invite parents to join your quarterly visit to a local nursing home or annual service day at your denominational camp. Also look for new possibilities like a shared small group series with parents and kids, or one-time events that take on a family-oriented flavor.

» Exploring opportunities that create shared, longer-duration experiences to which both parents and their children can refer back as significant moments. Family-based mission trips, retreats, and weeklong camps might seem like a small or huge step forward depending on your context, so be sure to start with less risky experiments before attempting something major.

» Preparing both parents and children to see the weekly worship experience as shared space where we all learn from (and need) each other. This may require a culture shift in your congregation beyond just parents and teen-agers, so please see Module 4 for more ideas on moving toward all-church worship without crashing and burning.

HELP ME BE A BETTER PARENT THROUGH BUILDING RELATIONAL NETWORKS

Parents commonly express a loneliness and busyness that comes with parent-ing. They need encouragement from other parents who are in the same boat. While we may pride ourselves in giving parents information, they also need friends who feel like they are paddling in the same direction (often upstream). While we probably shouldn't try to "assign" friendships, we can create spaces where these relationships emerge.

EXPLORE WAYS TO MEET THIS NEED BY:

» Hosting an annual conference on marriage and/or parenting for the par-ents in your community to attend and find connection.

» Offering short-term or long-term small group opportunities that allow par-ents in similar stages to have a shared and mutually supportive experience.

» Fostering a natural space for parents to connect with one another during regular youth ministry programming, or during the drop-off and pick-up windows when parents may tend to mill around the back of the youth room.

A SHARED DISCIPLESHIP EXPERIENCE CREATES OPPORTUNITIES FOR PARENTS TO APPROACH AN OTHERWISE ABSTRACT AND ANXIOUS TOPIC LIKE SPIRITUALITY IN A HANDS-ON WAY.

WHAT NOW?

1. Take a minute and reflect on your own impressions of the parents in your ministry. What assumptions have you made about some (or maybe all!) of them that may need to be reframed in order for you to engage them?
2. In Module 1, Part 5 we invited you to listen to parents and assess their view of the ministry. Depending on how thoroughly your team went about that task, this might be a good time to loop back and do some more listening.
3. As you listen, what themes keep surfacing? Resist trying to fit them into your vision or categories. Start by trying to articulate what parents are *really* saying.
4. What are some first steps you can take to respond to parents' needs in your context?
5. Catch a parent doing something right this week. Look for the small things. Cheer them on!

 LAUNCH TIP

"We've tried all kinds of ideas to connect with parents, but here's what we have found to generate the greatest engagement:

> » We *invite* parents to participate in ministry and provide a clear path toward becoming a volunteer in student ministry.
> » We *expect* the parent's first 'job' in the student ministry is to visit with and get to know students. We also clearly place the expectation for a student's growth at the feet of parents and other adult community members: I know we can't out-teach what happens in the home and surrounding adult community—we are not that good.
> » We *train* the parent volunteer with skills to understand today's teen culture and what it looks like to have 'relational wins' with teenagers.
> » We *celebrate* the role of parents in our student ministry. We constantly thank and brag about the parents who volunteer in our ministry. We provide times of prayer and support at major retreats and camps. We also host a yearly banquet in which we eat, have fun (babysitting provided), and share stories from the year."

DAVID FRAZE
DIRECTOR OF STUDENT MINISTRY
The Hills Church, Richland Hills, Texas

Part 2

HOW CAN I STRENGTHEN MY COMMUNICATION WITH PARENTS?

This might be hard to believe, but parents are "regular people." They have regular jobs, friendships, and very full calendars. Sometimes it feels like reaching out to them yields few results, and you may be inclined to give up. However, launching Sticky Faith at your church also means reaching into the home.

By now you know that what you announce at youth group may never make it to a parent's ears. You've heard parents bemoan that when they ask their teenager what the teaching was about, the answer is typically incoherent. If you rely solely on students to relay key information to their parents, the odds may not be in your favor.

At the same time, parents want to hear from you. The more you communicate with them about both vision and programming alike, the more they are able to be on your team. **When you take the initiative to stay in touch, you show that you value parents as part of your team.** The reverse is true as well: The less you communicate with parents about what you are doing and why you are doing it, the more difficult it is for them to give you their full support.

As we discussed in Part 1 of this module, it can be tempting to blame parents for this communication breakdown. *I'm here week after week. If they want to know more about what's going on, they can ask!* But given the nature of most parents' lives, that's just not realistic. What's more, parents may hesitate to take the first step if they think you might not welcome their questions.

> WHEN YOU TAKE THE INITIATIVE TO STAY IN TOUCH, YOU SHOW THAT YOU VALUE PARENTS AS PART OF YOUR TEAM.

WHAT NOW?

One simple but powerful approach to communicating with parents is sending consistent emails, which can allow you to introduce Sticky Faith concepts as well as to keep parents informed about other aspects of the youth ministry. Consistent emails give you the chance to communicate important information straight to parents. Email also gives them an easy channel by which to contact you. Parents can simply hit "reply" and share their thoughts or questions.

WHETHER OR NOT A PARENT'S RESPONSE IS RELATED TO THE CONTENT OF YOUR EMAIL IS NOT WHAT'S MOST IMPORTANT. EVERY RESPONSE FROM A PARENT OPENS THE DOOR FOR ENGAGEMENT.

CREATING A CONSISTENT PARENT EMAIL STRATEGY

If you do not already have a master family email list, build one. Here are some ideas to get started:

CHECK IN

For at least four weeks in a row, do a "check in" at the beginning of your gathering. The first week, ask students to fill out an information card as they arrive. The card should include their own information as well as their parents', and at the very least should request emails and phone numbers. Be sure to add at least two spots for parent contact information in order to account for divorced/remarried parents and students who live in multiple homes. (As a side note, this is also a great time to get birthday information so you can build that into your database as well. There's no day more special in kids' lives than their birthday, and a youth leader remembering is relational gold).

DATA

Each week, add the data into your church's database or a spreadsheet, and then print the student names from the spreadsheet to create a roster.

ATTENDANCE

For weeks two through four, students will either a) check their name off of the roster or b) fill out a card.

RAFFLE

If needed, motivate your students to complete a card with a simple raffle. During weeks two through four, give a ticket to each student as they check in. Give away candy or small gift cards to several winners. On the fifth week, raffle off a larger prize, drawing from all the names of students who completed info cards.

FOLLOW UP

At the end of this time you should have a good starter contact list for families, plus a system in place to gain new information as new students join your ministry. Whenever a new student shows up, you can hand him or her the information card and follow up not only with the student, but also his or her parents within a week after the first visit.

Once you have a contact list, set up a regular schedule for email updates. This may be weekly, bi-monthly, or once a month depending on your capacity. As a general rule, start with what you know you can consistently follow through with, even if that's only once a month. Once you decide, tell parents how often they can expect to hear from you. Following through with your promises—even about email—translates into increased credibility with parents (and vice versa). If you decide to send a weekly email, you may wish to alternate between writing about program updates one week and Sticky Faith themes the next.

Use clear headers, bullet point lists, and short paragraphs to help readers follow along easily. For example, a header that reads "8th Grade Promotion Party" tells parents of a sixth grader they can skip to the next section. Taking time to organize your message shows parents that you respect their time.

▶ INSTRUCTIONAL NOTE
"SAY WHAT?"

We almost hesitate to add this warning, but please proofread your email before you send it. We can't tell you how many times we've heard from parents that their youth leader's spelling and grammar are literary train wrecks. Your email doesn't need to be a masterpiece, but it does need to be clear and as error-free as possible.

LAUNCH TIP

"Our parents get Sticky Faith! They're really trying to raise their kids in community with each other. Our eighth grade parents in particular have built a community to disciple their kids together and it's been great. They do this primarily through bi-weekly family small groups. Along the way, we've done parent seminars and gatherings. We've involved more parents and adults as ministry leaders, chaperones, and Bible study small group leaders. We committed to communicate to parents every week through email and through a weekly blog, and it's really paid off in our level of connection."

TIM GALLEHER
PASTOR OF YOUTH AND FAMILY MINISTRIES
Saratoga Federated Church, Saratoga, California

STICKY FAITH TEMPLATES

To help you get started, we've created fourteen content templates you can adapt and include in parent emails. Each one introduces a Sticky Faith concept and invites parents to engage with the content. You might also want to add:

AN INTRODUCTORY HEADER

Top the email with a standard paragraph that explains how the email works. For example: "This is our weekly parent email, designed to keep you in the loop with our youth group. If you have any questions, please don't hesitate to reply and ask me. If you no longer wish to be on the email list for any reason, just let me know. I promise my feelings won't be hurt." Including a header gives context to people who are added into your list; putting it in italics cues regulars to just skip that part and go on to the next section.

UPCOMING EVENTS

It's especially helpful to include details like meeting location, time, cost, and an attachment or link to your release of liability or other registration forms.

WHAT YOU'RE TEACHING

Tell families what you're teaching about, and even offer a "car question" or two for them. In other words, what could parents ask their kids about your lesson beyond, "What'd you talk about today?" Set parents up for success, or at least for the possibility of hearing something beyond a grunt of, "Stuff," or, "I don't know."

REQUESTS FOR FEEDBACK

Ask parents for their input about things going on in the ministry. Generally, this works well if the questions are neutral (e.g., "What night of the week is best for your family for small groups this fall?" or "How late is too late for an event to end?") and the answers they would send back can be short. Be sure to leave the door open for other feedback or questions.

Below is the first of fourteen templates for you to use mostly as-is or to nuance based on your context. They all include some areas in brackets for you to fill in specific details, so please don't ever cut and paste into an email without reading it completely. If you find that you'd rather split some of this content into two emails, or print it in a paper newsletter you hand out or mail out, go for it. **You will find all of the email templates online for download and adaptation at stickyfaithlaunchkit.org.**

EMAIL 1:
AN INTRODUCTION TO STICKY FAITH

Hello Parents!

Welcome to our new [weekly, monthly, etc.] family email. Thank you for taking the time to connect a bit more with our ministry.

Did you know that research shows 40-50 percent of students from good youth groups and families will drift from God and the church after high school? As a youth pastor, I'm not satisfied with that. And I imagine you aren't either as a parent.

Imagine we lined up your child's class, shoulder to shoulder, and then numbered them off as ones and twos. Then we said to the ones, "Congratulations! As you head off to college, your faith will stick with you. You will stay connected to Jesus, to church life, and to spiritual practices like prayer and reading your Bible." But then we turned to the twos and said, "You guys ... eh, as you graduate, you're going to struggle. We know you're part of our church right now, but as you grow up, that won't be the case. Sorry about that."

It would break our hearts, of course.

Here at [church name], we have begun to reflect deeply on research from the Fuller Youth Institute about developing **Sticky Faith** in the lives of our students. We want your children to develop faith that sticks with them beyond youth group. We desire to help young people follow Jesus for a lifetime, and there are things we can do together to increase the likelihood that will happen.

Over the coming months, our team will focus on ways we can instill Sticky Faith in the lives of every one of our students. **As a parent you are essential to this process, and I want to invite you to be part of what we're doing.** Each week [or every other week, or once a month] I will send a short email introducing one concept from Sticky Faith, along with a question or two about what it means for us here at [church name]. I'm excited to see what God will do through this process in the lives of our students and families! If you want to learn more about Sticky Faith on your own, you can visit stickyfaith.org.

Think about that first statistic again: 40-50 percent of students from good youth groups and families will drift from God and the church after high school. How does that number make you feel? If you were to guess, what would you say are some key reasons young people choose to stick with or walk away from faith?

LAUNCH TIP

"Knowing that it can be hard for parents and teenagers to ask one another good questions, we send out lists of questions: 100 each for parents and for kids.[1] Some of the questions are tough; others might be awkward. We set up a few rules:

1. No answer is stupid. No grimacing, eye rolling, or in any way laughing at someone unless they are saying something funny.

2. Everyone gets to answer without interruption. Follow-up questions are allowed ("But I thought you liked beets!"), but follow-up answers aren't required.

3. Questions that hit a recent sore spot should be avoided if at all possible. For example, if your child has just missed making the team or been dumped by a major heartthrob, you might want to avoid those kinds of questions the first couple of times you try this out.

4. Everyone is, in fact, allowed to avoid two questions each time—more if they really insist upon it. This has to be fun, remember? Better to lose one answer than to lose their interest and engagement in the conversation."

JAY CLARK AND KATYE DUNN
YOUTH MINISTERS
Pulaski Heights United Methodist Church, Little Rock, Arkansas

▶ **INSTRUCTIONAL NOTE**
Download all fourteen email templates from stickyfaithlaunchkit.org and adapt them for your own parent email series. We've written topical emails on everything from parent-child communication to creating family rituals. We hope they will help you connect with parents without having to create lots of content yourself.

---

1   For good lists of questions, see familyeducation.com, especially "100 Questions to Ask Your Parents," http://life.fami-lyeducation.com/communication/family-time/36022.html, and "100 Questions to Ask Your Kids," http://life.familyed-ucation.com/communication/family-time/36021.html

Part 3

LEADING A STICKY FAITH PARENT SEMINAR

We often are asked by leaders like you, "How would you structure a parent meeting on Sticky Faith?"

Just for you, we've written up our answer!

The outline below includes main ideas and talking points for a sixty-to-ninety-minute parent training. **We suggest you plan this with your Launch Team for month three or four of your process,** once you've developed some stories of future hope (see Module 1, Part 6) and have become conversant on Sticky Faith yourself.

▶ **ADDITIONAL RESOURCES (BONUS!)**
Download a slide show in PowerPoint or Keynote to use with this parent seminar from stickyfaithlaunchkit.org. You'll look like a pro! Make sure you include pictures from your own church that illustrate some of the points in the seminar with relevant stories. Also make sure you think through technical details ahead of time, like connecting your computer to a sound system in order to play the videos. One of the ways you can show your competence to parents is to test everything out beforehand to show you've prepared well.

▶ **ADDITIONAL RESOURCES**
Some leaders have found it helpful to invite parents to read copies of *Sticky Faith: Everyday Ideas to Build Lasting Faith in Your Kids* (by Kara Powell and Chap Clark) as part of their launch strategy. Whether simply making the recommendation, handing out copies of the book, setting up a parent book club, or creating a parent small group series utilizing the *Sticky Faith Parent Curriculum DVD*, engaging parents in more Sticky Faith content will further your efforts toward change. The good news is that Zondervan Publishing is partnering with us on providing discounts to leaders like you who have purchased the Sticky Faith Launch Kit. Using the code "launchkit" at churchsource.com (or calling 1-800-727-3480) you can get a 30 percent discount on 1-5 copies, a 40 percent discount on 6-19 copies, and a 50 percent discount on 20 or more copies of any *Sticky Faith* resource for your congregation, plus free shipping for orders over $50.

HOW DO I MOTIVATE MORE PARENTS TO ATTEND OUR PARENT MEETINGS?

If we get asked that first question above a lot, we hear this second one even more. Especially when we talk about the importance of youth ministries and parents partnering together to impact teenagers, at least one hand predictably shoots into the air. We know this question is coming.

Usually our first response after someone asks that question is, "And isn't it true that the 10-20 percent of parents who show up are the ones who are already the most dialed in to your ministry and their own children, and they could probably be presenting the training themselves?"

Heads nod all around the room.

It seems to us that there are a lot of reasons parents don't come: they're busy, maybe they feel like their kids are already in high school so it's too late, or perhaps previous parent training events haven't been that helpful.

But here's one that might be more common than we might think: We as leaders don't promote them as well as we could and should. We assume that if we send out one (or maybe two) letter(s) or email(s), the job of promotion is done.

That's why we were so encouraged by a recent email from a student ministry pastor when we asked him how his team was going to be promoting a parent training event in four weeks. Here is the list of ways they are promoting that event at their church:

» Announcements will be included in the worship folder at worship services for four weeks.
» Separate email newsletters will go out to preteen, junior high, and high school parents just about this event.
» The weekly children's ministry parent e-newsletter will highlight the training.
» Announcements and flyers will be in every adult and children's Sunday school class the week prior to the training.
» The ministry staff will be blogging about it a week ahead of time.
» The church's Facebook page will promote the event for ten days leading up to it.
» Each volunteer will contact six to eight parents two weeks ahead of time, asking them to contact two more parents and invite them to the event.

WE AS LEADERS DON'T PROMOTE PARENT EVENTS AS WELL AS WE COULD AND SHOULD.

We love how this student ministry team is being so proactive. We've heard from other teams that have involved students in the process of inviting parents by texting students the morning of the event so they will remind their parents. We know another church that had a big balloon display at church the Sunday morning of their parent training as a reminder to those parents who intend to go to training but, once they arrive at church, slip into their normal patterns and go to their regular class instead.

You know your church culture best. You know what your parents tend to respond to and what they don't. So please craft your own communication plan based on what you already know. But if you're one of those leaders who often mopes about parent attendance following a sparse event, perhaps you could pepper your communication strategy with one or more of these ideas.

SEMINAR OUTLINE

▶ **INSTRUCTIONAL NOTE**
Please adapt this outline based on your context and time available. Feel free to add your own stories or examples from your life and church. This is just a suggested starting point based on the main principles of Sticky Faith. For further explanation of these main points and the research behind them, please read *Sticky Faith: Youth Worker Edition*.

I   INTRODUCTION
II   SHIFT #1
III   SHIFT #2
IV   SHIFT #3
V   AND FINALLY ...

I. INTRODUCTION
YOUNG PEOPLE ARE WALKING AWAY FROM FAITH

1.1   Research shows that 40-50 percent of students from good youth groups and families will drift from God and the church after high school. That's like lining up the kids in our youth ministry or in your family and counting them off by ones and twos. The "ones" will stick with faith and the "twos" will walk away. As leaders and as parents, none of us want that to be the case for our kids.

1.2   We want to show you this brief video of interviews with college students about their experience of faith after high school.

 ▶ **VIDEO**
Show the video "Faith After High School" here, either embedded in the slide show or another way. Download the file from stickyfaithlaunchkit.org.

DEBRIEF QUESTIONS FOLLOWING THE VIDEO:
» What stood out to you most in this video?
» What similar or different experiences do you think young people from our church experience after high school?
» What fears and hopes does this video raise for you?

1.3   In order to understand more about what helps faith stick into young adulthood, the Fuller Youth Institute studied over 500 youth group graduates for three years across the transition out of high school. Their research uncovered three main shifts that are needed in order to help young people develop a faith that sticks. We're in the midst of working through what this looks like in our own context here at our church. (At this point you might want to briefly describe your timeline and introduce your Launch Team so folks know who they can talk to with ideas and concerns).

II. SHIFT #1
FROM A BEHAVIOR-BASED GOSPEL TO A GRACE-BASED GOSPEL

2.1   When the Fuller Youth Institute asked youth group graduates three years after high school to describe what it means to be a Christian, the most common responses didn't mention Jesus; they mentioned "loving people." While loving others is a great way to practice faith, the problem comes in seeing faith primarily as something we *do* to please God. When many young people think about faith, they think about a list of behaviors. They believe God will like them better if they can follow a list of "Do's and Don'ts" based on keeping their sin in check. This type of faith is analogous to a jacket; it can be put on and taken off, but it doesn't change what's on the inside.

▶ **INSTRUCTIONAL NOTE**
You may want to wear a jacket for the opening of the seminar, taking it off during this point as an illustration of faith.

When students with this type of faith experience some sort of failure in high school or college, they feel like they've taken off their faith (like a jacket) and thrown it into a corner. As parents, we can help our kids develop a more robust understanding of the gospel—one that integrates faith into all of life and knows that Jesus is bigger than any mistake. If Jesus can't handle our failures, we need a bigger Jesus.

2.2 One way we've found helpful in describing the gospel to adults and students alike is using the 5-G model. This is based on Reformation theology but adapted to add the first "G," Good and the fourth "G," God's People.

> » **GOOD:** God created us good, in God's image.
> » **GUILT:** We then chose to disobey God, leaving us with the guilt of sin. All of us carry this mark and it impacts us every day.
> » **GRACE:** Through the life, death, and resurrection of Jesus, God has extended grace to us to make things right and restore us to relationship with God and one another.
> » **GOD'S PEOPLE:** As we experience grace, we are adopted into the body of Christ, embodying God's reign in the world. We join the mission of God, participating in the work of God happening through God's people.
> » **GRATITUDE:** Out of this gift of grace, we respond in gratitude toward God. *This* is the well out of which our obedience—those behaviors—flows. In other words, the Sticky Gospel doesn't begin with behaviors, nor is it dependent on behaviors. Our behaviors are like a big thank-you note we offer back to God in response to grace. As we grow in trust, we naturally grow in obedience as a response to grace.

2.3 We can learn to model this gospel for our kids by centering our family relationships and interactions in grace. (This is a great place for a story or two in your own life about the power of grace.) This doesn't mean we don't set boundaries for our kids or discipline them when they break those boundaries. It means that we're willing to remind our kids that Jesus' love—and ours—is bigger than any mistake. The mistakes don't define us as much as our identity in Christ. This is also true for us as parents. Sometimes we need to ask for our kids' forgiveness for our mistakes too.

TALK ABOUT IT

If you are doing a ninety-minute or two-hour seminar, get parents talking here in groups of three or four with this prompt: "Think of a recent situation in which offering grace was a real struggle. Brainstorm options for responding where grace and restoration play more of a part."

III. SHIFT #2
FROM A TWO-TABLE CHURCH TO A CHURCH THAT WELCOMES YOUNG PEOPLE AROUND ONE FAMILY TABLE

3.1   FYI research shows that intergenerational worship and relationships are linked with faith that sticks. Out of thirteen different participation variables (like church attendance, being part of a small group, etc.), intergenerational connections were some of the strongest predictors of Sticky Faith. The problem is that many of our students don't know the church at all; they only know the youth group. The better we get at youth ministry, the more we tend to segregate students, much like an adults' table and a kids' table at a family gathering.

3.2   While we're not calling for an end to youth ministry, we're calling for a new approach in which the whole church finds more ways to come around one table as a faith family. Ideally each young person is surrounded by a team of five adults who consistently support and walk with them. We call this a new 5:1 ratio for ministry.

That doesn't mean five small group leaders for every student, but rather a team of five adults who include mentors, coaches, teachers, or even adults in the church who simply know their name and are praying for them. Research from the Search Institute shows that the more adults who know a kids' name, the more likely that kid is to thrive in all areas of life.[1] What if we started that here in our church?

3.3   There's a lot our youth ministry and entire church could do to increase this 5:1 ratio. Some of the ideas other churches have experimented with include intergenerational worship, mentoring, service/mission trips, small groups, and other activities. Often this doesn't mean adding more programs, but looking at what already exists in a church and finding opportunities for more synergy across generations. (At this point, please add some of your own observations and ideas about your own church.)

---

1   Read more about Search's research on Developmental Assets at http://www.search-institute.org/research/developmental-assets

3.4   Ideally, parents can lead the way in developing this kind of web around their kids. Our role in the youth ministry can be to support and create opportunities for more connections, but ideally you would be the catalyst. Chances are good that your kids already have a few of those five adults in place in their lives. As a family, start with your friends, extended family members, other adults who already care (like teachers and coaches), and adults you know your kids like. You might even start by asking your kids directly what adults they really admire and enjoy being with.

TALK ABOUT IT

IF YOU HAVE ENOUGH TIME, INVITE PARENTS TO GET INTO PAIRS TO DISCUSS THESE QUESTIONS:

» Where do we already have intergenerational relationships in our family? our church?

» What ideas do we have for starting to build a web of 5:1 adults in our family? our church?

IV. SHIFT #3
FROM "DRY-CLEANER PARENTING" TO MINISTRY PARTNERSHIP

4.1   Often youth ministry feeds into a "dry-cleaner parenting" model. Dry-cleaner parents drop their kids off at youth group expecting to pick them up ninety minutes later all clean and pressed. In other words, they've learned to outsource their kids' spiritual development. (Here's a good time to confess to parents that you've been part of this movement. This is NOT a good time to point a finger of blame at parents for participating.)

4.2   Yet, as one researcher has said, "When it comes to faith, parents tend to get what they are."[2] In other words, the faith of parents is actually one of the best predictors of the faith of kids as young adults. That might either be exciting or scary to you. Of course there are exceptions. Kids make their own choices, and sometimes kids from committed Christian families run away from God. But in general, parents still have the most influence on faith—even through the teenage years.

4.3   Here are a few ideas from the Fuller Youth Institute to help support what you're already doing or begin something new:

> » FAITH CONVERSATIONS
> Most families actually don't talk much about faith at home, but research shows that having conversations about faith leads to more mature faith in young people. The best conversations happen informally and include parents sharing about their own faith, not just interrogating kids about what happened at youth group.

> » SHARING YOUR SPIRITUAL JOURNEY
> Do your kids know your testimony of how you became a follower of Jesus? Do they know why you still follow Jesus today? Knowing that narrative can strengthen your kids' own narrative of faith.

---

2   Christian Smith summarizing research from the National Study of Youth and Religion in a panel at Fuller Seminary, March 2008. Also see Christian Smith with Melinda Lundquist Denton, *Soul Searching: The Religious and Spiritual Lives of American Teenagers* (New York: Oxford Press, 2005), 56.

» SERVING TOGETHER
Families who serve others together tend to grow in faith together. Whether it's joining a church-sponsored opportunity or finding your family's own way to reach out to those in need, serving can open up all kinds of doors for growth. Find at least one way your family can start serving together.

4.4 Talk about it. Here we suggest holding a large-group conversation and Q&A time in which you share one or two of the next steps your team has identified for helping families nurture Sticky Faith in their kids. Invite ideas parents have from their own families' experiences, and ask for input on how to strengthen the partnership between parents and the youth ministry. You may want to give them a way to write down suggestions and concerns (e.g., on index cards) and submit these at the end of the meeting, rather than launch a full parent critique session.

WHAT ABOUT PARENTS WHO AREN'T INVOLVED OR AREN'T BELIEVERS?

We get this question a lot from leaders, and you'll likely hear it from the parents who are committed enough to actually show up for your parent meeting too. We have two suggestions:

1. ANY POINT OF CONTACT IS A WIN
Whether you're able to get them on your email list (see Module 3, Part 2), meet one-on-one (see Module 3, Part 4), or catch them in the parking lot as they're picking up their kids, consider it a win and an opportunity to build a friendship.

2. UTILIZE ENGAGED PARENTS TO REACH OUT
Your best advocates and best natural connection to an uninvolved parent is an involved one. Invite some of your enthusiastic parents to reach out in person or by phone or email to parents who are on the fringes. It may be enough to open up a new conversation.

I AM THE VINE; YOU ARE THE BRANCHES. IF YOU REMAIN IN ME AND I IN YOU, YOU WILL BEAR MUCH FRUIT; APART FROM ME YOU CAN DO NOTHING.

JOHN 15:5

V. AND FINALLY ...
CLOSE IN PRAYER

Close in prayer—for your students, their families, and your church family. You might want to read a passage of scripture like John 15:5: "I am the vine; you are the branches. If you remain in me and I in you, you will bear much fruit; apart from me you can do nothing."

▶ INSTRUCTIONAL NOTE
BONUS TIP
Email parents a few days after the seminar to ask for further feedback and any questions that have popped up in the meantime. This can be a great way to leverage the momentum of meeting in person and learn more about how they've been processing what you shared.

🚀 LAUNCH TIP

"We hosted 'Sticky Faith Parent Classes,' going through the *Sticky Faith* parent book as a group and journeying through what Sticky Faith means for families at our church. Many identified changes they wanted to make. From those incredible conversations came opportunities for us to learn what we needed to change.

We find that this approach creates a better atmosphere for discussion on organizational change, because parents are not on the defensive, looking for someone to blame for the dysfunction in their family. They find themselves on the offensive, looking for ways to build a 5:1 ratio for their kids and surround their kids with positive influences and opportunities. Another big win is our 'Pastor-Parent Conferences.' This has created an intentional space where we invite parents to ask questions, pose concerns, and communicate about what happens in their family rhythm. Parents have appreciated us taking the time to listen, and it has gone a long way in helping parents see that we truly do care."

NATE ROSKAM
COMMUNITY LIFE PASTOR
Nampa First Nazarene, Nampa, Idaho

Part 4

SETTING UP "PARENT-LEADER CONFERENCES"

"We say we're always available to parents, but we're realizing that claim is kind of hollow."

This confession from a youth leader in one of our Sticky Faith Cohorts has been echoed by countless leaders as they take a good look at how they *actually* engage parents.

WE SAY WE'RE ALWAYS AVAILABLE TO PARENTS, BUT WE'RE REALIZING THAT CLAIM IS KIND OF HOLLOW.

While they might be pretty good at communicating via email, they rarely initiate a personal conversation with parents or sit down to talk face-to-face.

One solution to making your team more proactively available is to offer yearly one-on-one conferences between leaders and parents.[1]

 ## LAUNCH TIP

"We knew that if we could connect more deeply with parents, the likelihood of their children sticking with faith would increase. But after a few first attempts, we noticed that the same families attended every event we hosted. We were unable to reach new families or convince disengaged parents that this mattered. It was frustrating.

Taking our cue from schools, we started offering annual parent-leader conferences. We were a little nervous about whether parents would respond, but we were surprised when so many parents signed up the first year. What's more, we've been surprised by how this response has grown each year. It's becoming one of the major hallmarks of our student ministry."

JEFF MATTESICH
PASTOR OF FAMILIES AND YOUTH
Lake Avenue Church, Pasadena, California

We've heard this idea repeated in a number of churches, and it's become one of the Sticky Faith strategies we often recommend to leaders. Here are a handful of practices you might want to consider if you offer parent conferences in your ministry.

---

1   This section was adapted from an article by Jeff Mattesich for the FYI E-Journal entitled, "Parent Conferences: Five Ideas for 1-1 Meetings." See http://fulleryouthinstitute.org/articles/parent-conferences.

FIVE IDEAS FOR ONE-ON-ONE MEETINGS

 ELIMINATE DISTRACTIONS AND MIXED MESSAGES
If you simply add these conferences alongside everything else you normally do, they won't seem like a priority and will get lost in the shuffle. Consider offering the conferences during a two-week period and shutting down as many of your normal programs as possible. This allows for the priority and emphasis to be clear to families. It says, "THIS IS REALLY IMPORTANT." This approach also frees you and your leaders to give your focus to parents more intentionally during this window.

 BE AVAILABLE TO MEET A VARIETY OF FAMILIES AND SCHEDULES
Although some parents can meet during the weekdays, many parents are only available on the weeknights and weekends. This means that those who lead the conferences may work a lot during this two-week season, but the time investment pays dividends down the road.

Churches have also found that giving a clear time expectation is helpful to parents. Thirty minutes is a good general rule of thumb. It's inviting without being too intimidating for parents who aren't as connected. Give parents options to sign up online through a meeting scheduling website or by calling to set up a time.

 STICK TO THE PROMISED TIME
There will be plenty of parents who will want to spend the entire day with you, but the majority of parents will want to stick to what was advertised. You can always set up an additional meeting if they have other things they want to discuss. Sometimes you'll need to remind them that this is about their child and not an open forum on their likes and dislikes of the youth ministry. By sticking to the shorter meeting, you can better guide the time.

THE CONTENT OF THE MEETING MUST BE BOTH GENERAL AND PERSONAL
You might begin by talking for the first part of the conference. Share your ministry philosophy and the values that drive your calendar. Give them areas where their involvement is most needed, but don't make this about volunteer recruitment. The goal is to help parents gain an overall understanding of why you exist and what an ideal partnership looks like, and also to share a vision that is less overwhelming for un-churched families or those whose lives are overscheduled. That leaves the second half of the meeting for a discussion about that particular family. Invite parents to share anything you need to know about their family, the student, or experiences that might help you minister to them and meet their needs. These times have proven to be very powerful, as families often seem free to share things they have not shared before. Your role at this point is to reassure them, grieve with them, celebrate with them, and always pray with them. Parents often feel so alone in parenting. You can help them feel more normal and remind them that you are on their side.

 BE REDUNDANT
Think ahead of time with your team about the main message you want to communicate to parents. For example, explain that your team wants to support and partner with parents in the faith journey of their teenage kids. Repeat this goal over and over; open with it, transition with it, and end with it.

One issue that often arises when we share about these conferences is student confidentiality. How do we balance both respecting the student and sharing important insights with parents? If you know something specific that is a struggle area for a student, then that information needs to be handled sensitively in the context of the meeting. A good general rule is: Don't share something a student has shared confidentially with you unless the student or others are at risk of harm.

You may find that only paid staff members can lead these parent conferences, mainly because of schedule constraints. If that is the case, it's a good idea to consult with a volunteer who is particularly close to the student prior to the meeting (e.g., their small group leader).

The way this parent conference strategy plays out in your ministry may look different from the five ideas shared here. Make it your own, and adapt it to your context. You might just discover that parent conferences become a significant part of your ministry to families.

Part 5

CREATING FAITH MILESTONES

Growing up is hard. So is parenting those who are growing up.

Maybe that's why we celebrate the markers along the way that remind us all we're one leg farther along the journey. These markers could be the first day of kindergarten, the last day of elementary school, and high school graduation. Outside of school, memorable experiences like a first date, earning a driver's license, or bringing home a first paycheck from a part-time job can all evoke reminders that childhood isn't forever. These events raise all kinds of feelings for both parents and kids.

One way we can serve families on the Sticky Faith journey is by setting up rites of passage that mark specific milestones along the way.[1] These life and faith markers can provide critical windows for engaging families at particularly tender times.

Throughout the history of God's people detailed in the Old Testament, significant encounters with God were often marked by building altars.[2] For example, take Jacob, who wrestled with God through the night and then built an altar to remember what God had done in his life. The altar stands as a tangible sign of a spiritual event. We call those signs "faith milestones."

As you partner with families, help parents consider the milestones that already exist in their families, as well as new rituals they might develop. Explore together rites of passage within your church, like baptism, confirmation, or other transitions (more ideas on this below). These markers can act as a concrete map of hoped-for faith development that fuels parents' and the church's involvement in the lives of young people.

You might begin with conversations with your Launch Team about what rites of passage might look like in your context. One church began this journey by asking: *What does faith development look like in our community from birth to when our young people leave for college and beyond?*

---

1   The term "rites of passage" was coined by French anthropologist Arnold Van Gennep, explaining significant community rituals that shape young people's identity. For more on understanding rites of passage in the youth ministry context, see Brad Griffin, http://stickyfaith.org/articles/through-the-zone.

2   Parts of this section are adapted from an online article by Steven Johnson for the FYI E-Journal entitled "Milestones of Faith: Creating rhythms through rites of passage," http://stickyfaith.org/articles/milestones-of-faith.

A FIRST RITE OF PASSAGE: BAPTISM OR INFANT DEDICATION

In many Christian communities, infants are dedicated or baptized into faith by their parents and their community. Within the ceremony parents and/or sponsors are asked to promise before God and the community that they will raise their kids in the faith. They respond with something like, "Yes, with the help of God."

The pastor then turns while holding the baby and presents the child to the church community. The pastor asks the community, "Will you commit to praying for this child and for the parents, and to helping raise the child in the faith?" The congregation is then urged to respond, "Yes, with the help of God."

> WITH THIS CEREMONY, A CHILD BECOMES A PART OF THE FAITH FAMILY.

With this ceremony, a child becomes a part of the faith family. As the first of many milestones in a child's spiritual journey, baptism or infant dedication gives the congregation a chance to equip parents, as well as the community, to pour into each child. Consider ways to make this moment even more meaningful by adding some or all of the following elements:

TRAIN

Train parents ahead of time. Some churches make this a prerequisite of infant baptism or dedication. The training may include specifics about what baptism means within your particular tradition, education about what ministries and programs your church offers to families with young children, and an opportunity to write a special letter to their child that will be kept until a later milestone like confirmation (see below), depending on your tradition.

CONNECT

Take the opportunity to connect with parents about their own faith journeys, past and present. Often the experience of giving birth or adopting a child can stir deep spiritual longings in a parent. By asking a few questions, you may open the door to deeper faith conversations.

LINK

Link new parents with mentor parents who are farther down the road. Whether this represents a short-term or long-term commitment, wisdom from older parents can boost families' confidence and increase their skill set. More than anything, experienced parents can help normalize many of the fearful and anxiety-producing elements of parenting.

BE HOLISTIC

Create a ceremony in which the whole congregation can remember their baptism. Examples include reciting a liturgy that reaffirms baptismal vows for everyone present or offering the opportunity to receive the mark of the cross with oil on each person's forehead.

FOLLOW UP

Follow up with participating families within a week by email, offering to get together to talk more about faith development, and sharing your Sticky Faith vision for all kids within the congregation. Be sure to give specific details about available classes, groups, or other ways to connect.

ADDING DEVELOPMENTAL MILESTONES FROM ELEMENTARY TO HIGH SCHOOL

Some churches have approached milestones by designing a formational arc from early childhood through the end of high school. This pathway guides their work at each age level beyond the ebb and flow of particular curriculum series or short-term themes. If you consider something like this in your context, you will likely want to begin with what's most natural: the faith celebrations already present in your community. From there, wonder together with your Launch Team (and perhaps with parents) about other tools to equip parents and loop in the entire community as young people experience major milestones along the way.

 ## LAUNCH TIP

"We asked ourselves: *What do we want kids and families to learn during this stage of their life?* Around this question we built developmentally appropriate learning goals and then milestones for each grade level. For example, when a child enters into second grade we want them to start to grasp the importance of the Bible in their faith development. We introduced a milestone focused on the Bible. At the beginning of that second grade year, parents attend a class on the importance of reading the Bible to their kids and helping their kids start to read their own Bibles. Then during a Sunday service, families are brought forward and the parents are given Bibles. The parents then hand the Bibles to their own kids and make a promise in front of the church to read the Word of God together. Throughout the school year, kids are encouraged to bring their Bibles to Sunday school so that they can learn how to read and learn from them."

STEVEN JOHNSON
DIRECTOR OF STUDENT MINISTRIES
Good Shepherd Lutheran Church, Irvine, California

WONDER TOGETHER
WITH YOUR LAUNCH
TEAM (AND PERHAPS
WITH PARENTS)
ABOUT OTHER TOOLS
TO EQUIP PARENTS
AND LOOP IN THE
ENTIRE COMMUNITY
AS YOUNG PEOPLE
EXPERIENCE MAJOR
MILESTONES ALONG
THE WAY.

Below are ideas from real churches for each grade level. Consider which of these milestones and rites of passage might make sense in your context, but please don't try to incorporate everything all at once! **A good first step may be gathering with your Launch Team to think through the faith journey you hope young people take through the school-age years.** If your Launch Team hasn't included parents or anyone from other age-level ministries (e.g., elementary, college), now is the perfect time to weave them into the conversation. By their nature, milestones should be developed in partnership with the other ministry areas involved in the transition, and alongside parents.

CONSIDER WHICH OF THESE MILESTONES AND RITES OF PASSAGE MIGHT MAKE SENSE IN YOUR CONTEXT.

ELEMENTARY MILESTONE EXAMPLES

KINDERGARTEN: THE LORD'S PRAYER
Children learn the Lord's Prayer and explore what it means. They learn that prayer is communication with God and something they can participate in even as kids. At the end of the series, kids recite the prayer by memory and the church prays the prayer together alongside them as a community.

FIRST GRADE: JOHN 3:16
During Sunday school, students begin to learn the basic idea of the gospel. Families work with their kids to understand this concept over dinner conversations, with prompts from the children's ministry team.

SECOND GRADE: FIRST BIBLE
Each child's parent(s) presents their child with a children's Bible at the beginning of the year during a worship service. Then kids are invited to learn how to use it all year long in Sunday school as they journey through the Bible narrative. Parents also attend a class on the role of the Bible in the faith development of children, with tips on how to read the Bible with kids.

THIRD GRADE: FIRST COMMUNION
Parents and kids attend a special class that teaches kids the meaning of the Lord's Supper. Then at a special ceremony during worship, parents serve their kids communion for the first time. *This will vary based on your particular tradition's perspective on the Lord's Supper.*

FOURTH GRADE: THE TEN COMMANDMENTS
Kids learn the meaning of the "law" and the context of the Ten Commandments through the teaching of the children's ministry. At the end of the year, they recite the Ten Commandments by memory. This is coupled with teaching on grace that covers our inability to keep these commandments or be "good enough" for God, and Jesus' work to restore us to relationship with God.

FIFTH GRADE: THE APOSTLE'S CREED
Each family receives a copy of the Apostle's Creed as kids start to learn more about the meaning of their faith and the teaching of the Apostle's Creed with their families.

MIDDLE SCHOOL MILESTONE EXAMPLES

SIXTH GRADE: YOUTH BIBLE

Students each receive a new youth Bible as they enter middle school ministry. This may be an opportunity for another community rite of passage based around blessing students as they embark on adolescence and a new phase of encountering scripture with rapidly changing brains and bodies.

SEVENTH GRADE: TRADITION-SPECIFIC TEACHING

Kids begin to explore the distinctive features of their particular denomination/tradition and the leaders who formed the movement (e.g., Martin Luther, John Wesley, John Calvin).

EIGHTH GRADE: CONFIRMATION

This varies quite a bit from tradition to tradition, but "confirmation" is a rite of passage in which young people publicly affirm the faith that has been largely claimed for them by their parents and community up until this point. In some cases, children were baptized as infants and this ceremony is a way to remember and claim for themselves the faith promises made on their behalf. In other cases, confirmation includes the rite of baptism. Churches take anywhere from a few weeks to a few years to prepare young people for confirmation, and ceremonies might include public sharing by students and specific prayers by parents and community members. Confirmation processes infused with Sticky Faith also typically include some form of parent classes or training, as well as matching students with mentors from the congregation who support and pray for them during the process.

LAUNCH TIP

"In our denomination confirmation is a big step in helping young people explore and own their faith. It consists of several weeks of training about who Jesus is, spiritual gifts, church history, and other topics that help students explore their faith. The goal is for every student to understand what his or her faith is about before joining the church.

I've seen many students come through the class, join the church, and never get connected to the student ministry or the church body. They drop out after their confirmation experience in middle school. On Senior Sunday, those same students come back and stand in front of the church when they're about to go off to college or into the work world. I know they really don't have a church home to come back to at all.

This began to burden our hearts as a staff, and we began to talk about how we could stop the bleed-out that takes place every year following confirmation. We decided to try something different with confirmation:

>> We rewrote the curriculum in an attempt to make connecting with Jesus the most important topic we cover.

>> We added a **small group component** to confirmation so that students are connected with two adults in the church other than their parents.

>> We also added a **parent component** to the class designed to equip parents to talk to their kids about faith. One of our pastors led a parent class and taught parents the material the students would learn the next week so that they were ready to have discussions at home.

>> Finally, we added a **family week** to the curriculum. We canceled confirmation class that Sunday and asked parents to lead the discussion at home. For their at-home 'assignment' we wrote some conversation prompts and trained them ahead of time in the parent class. We encouraged both parents and students to create a timeline from birth to their current age and add significant personal and spiritual milestones along the way. The goal was to reflect on and share their journeys with one another.

We were excited about creating an environment where faith talks could happen naturally. Guess what happened: The students came back actually knowing their parents' stories, having new insights into milestones in their own faith journeys, and having had the opportunity to share their own testimonies with their parents."

LAUREN EDEN
STUDENT MINISTRY ASSOCIATE
Mt Bethel United Methodist, Atlanta, Georgia

ONE CHURCH WE KNOW SETS OUT A JOURNAL FOR EACH GRADUATING SENIOR FOR THE FEW WEEKS LEADING UP TO THIS SUNDAY. CONGREGATION MEMBERS FILL THE PAGES WITH AFFIRMATIONS, MEMORIES, HOPES, AND PRAYERS.

HIGH SCHOOL MILESTONE EXAMPLES

NINTH GRADE: DISCIPLESHIP

High school ministry begins to focus on discipleship that will prepare young people with faith they will carry into adulthood. This may mean revisiting most of what the earlier ministries have taught up to this point, recognizing that this new developmental phase carries with it new layers of questions. One church's goal in this stage is to place each new high school student in a discipleship group that will last for the rest of high school, in an attempt to provide consistent community and support.

TENTH GRADE: GIFTING

Offer students a spiritual gifts series that will help them discern how their passions, natural gifting, and spiritual gifts work together as God's calling to serve the world. Try to place each student in roles in your church serving alongside adults in order to explore gifting and calling.

ELEVENTH GRADE: RETREAT

Recognizing that this is typically the most intense year of high school, one church intentionally plans two spiritual retreats that encourage students to pause and reflect along the way. An additional goal of the retreats is to help young people develop intentional spiritual disciplines that will help prepare them to carry faith beyond high school.

▶ **ADDITIONAL RESOURCES**

We wrote a curriculum to use with juniors and seniors as they prepare for life after high school. You can use your Launch Kit discount to purchase the *Sticky Faith Teen Curriculum* at 30 percent off! Enter the code "launchkit" at churchsource.com when you place your order.

TWELFTH GRADE: COMMISSIONING

Develop a monthly class for seniors to help them think through their spiritual life after high school. At the end of the year, students invite friends and family to a barbecue celebration honoring all seniors. During this time, seniors thank friends and family for helping them develop as a Christian, and seniors are invited to share testimonies of their spiritual journeys. On the following Sunday, the church community commissions students into the next phase of life in a special ceremony. One church we know sets out a journal for each graduating senior for the few weeks leading up to this Sunday. Congregation members fill the pages with affirmations, memories, hopes, and prayers. The young people are presented with the journals as part of the church's blessing and commissioning.

LAUNCH TIP

"At our church, milestones became a big focus of our Sticky Faith plan. We began thinking about milestones in a few main categories below. Our goal is to try to celebrate each milestone both corporately and individually:

1. PERSONAL GROWTH PLANS
All middle school and high school students individually complete a personal growth plan to focus on for the upcoming year and then share the plan with their small group. The plans consist of writing out four goals for spiritual growth for the year.

2. STORIES OF FUTURE HOPE
Students write their own stories of future hope. Dreaming about their next few years and what their lives will look like in light of their faith, they write out those stories and share them with their small group leaders. Last year, different students shared their future hope stories with the entire group each week during student ministry program nights.

3. WE TRY TO CELEBRATE POSITIVE MILESTONES IN ADVANCE
We no longer want church to be the last place students celebrate life events like graduation or school promotion, so we try to more intentionally schedule advance celebrations rather than trailing after the fact.

4. WE TRY TO BE EQUIPPED FOR DIFFICULT MILESTONES WHEN THEY HAPPEN
We don't just look at positive rituals coming from our church tradition. We also try to prepare for rites of passage that are difficult life experiences. As much as we attempt to equip young people to make good decisions ahead of time, sometimes we have to deal with a rite of passage that may have painful repercussions, like a pregnancy, an expulsion from school, or a trip to jail. We've had small group leaders in delivery rooms with teenage moms and have visited students in juvenile detention centers. Along the way we've recognized that young people need our faithful presence during these hard milestones too.

5. WE TRY TO MAKE MILESTONES INTERGENERATIONAL

For seniors we have graduation Sunday, but we also take a senior camping trip where adults across the generations join us to share life wisdom. We've started connecting incoming sixth graders with adult mentors to serve in the church in a specific area for the year.

6. WE TRY TO INVOLVE PARENTS IN DIFFERENT MILESTONES

We do this through scheduling parenting classes, offering resources, communicating frequently during transition times, and being accessible for parents' questions and needs in these seasons."

MATTHEW DEPREZ
INTERGENERATIONAL PASTOR
Frontline Community Church, Grand Rapids, MI

WHAT NOW?

DETERMINE YOUR GOALS FOR FAITH DEVELOPMENT

Your church probably has a set of faith experiences or learning goals you hope kids will grasp, whether you have articulated them or not. With your Launch Team, map out those hopes for children and teenagers in your congregation. Make sure to consider developmental abilities at different ages. *What are the core aspects of faith we want kids in our community to understand and engage at each stage of childhood and adolescence? What's most important to parents and families?*

CREATE MILESTONES BASED ON YOUR GOALS

Develop a few age-specific or experience-specific milestones that match your congregation's culture and hopes for young people. Eventually you might want to create programs to support these milestones. Look for ways to involve families in this development phase. *What might specific milestones look like in our community? What other factors do we need to consider as we shape them? Who else needs to be involved?*

ENGAGE FAMILIES AND THE COMMUNITY IN MILESTONES

One of the hallmarks of Sticky Faith is that the faith development of young people requires the entire church. *What might it look like for our church to be involved in each milestone? What opportunities for intergenerational connection exist?*

EXPERIMENT ON THE MARGINS

Starting small is okay. Consider incorporating one new milestone per year, or one in each age-level ministry, rather than flooding your congregation with new expectations and rituals all at once. *What are natural first milestones that fit with our congregation right now? How could we set these up well, and how will we know afterward if the milestone was a success?*

WHERE ARE WE, AGAIN?

At this point you might be feeling a bit overwhelmed by ideas. Take a few deep breaths and remember that this is a marathon, not a sprint. Now is a good time to check back in with your Breakthrough Plan (Module 1, Part 8) and assess your stated goals based on your Launch Team's work. How can some of the ideas or tools in this module best help you accomplish your goals? What new ideas do you want to consider incorporating into your plan?

As a reminder, each module in this series is designed to be a reference point you can return to over and over. You might want to loop back to Module 1 for help with thinking about the change process. You might be eager to move to Module 4 on how to engage the whole church. Or you might take a step back to Module 2 and consider how to bring volunteers up to speed on new ideas you have for equipping parents. Flip back and forth as necessary!

> AT THIS POINT YOU MIGHT BE FEELING A BIT OVERWHELMED BY IDEAS. TAKE A FEW DEEP BREATHS AND REMEMBER THAT THIS IS A MARATHON, NOT A SPRINT.

MODULE 04

TAKING STICKY FAITH TO THE WHOLE CHURCH

Part 1

WHY DO I NEED THE WHOLE CHURCH?

LAUNCH TIP

"Our congregation is dedicated to breaking up the silos of traditional ministry programming. As a whole church we want to partner with families (no matter the degree of function or dysfunction) in the spiritual formation of young people. Because of this, students are welcome and fully-functioning participants on church ministry teams, worship leading, technical and fine arts crews, teaching roles in children and student programming, and other traditionally 'adult-only' areas of church life. Here are a few things we have used to keep this Sticky Faith energy and commitment strong:

» We have created rites of passage that involve the entire community of faith. These are major Sticky Faith moments that continue to be great wins for all ages.

» Once a year, I preach a 'Sticky Sermon' to the church body. This typically happens at the beginning of each school year and highlights the roles of the church and the family in the spiritual formation of young people.

» Our senior pastor uses a language of inclusion when speaking about student ministry programming. For instance, when our pastor speaks on missions, he highlights both student and adult projects with the same level of importance and excitement."

DAVID FRAZE
DIRECTOR OF STUDENT MINISTRY
The Hills Church, Richland Hills, Texas

We recently heard about a pastor who read *Sticky Faith*. When asked about his thoughts on the book by a ministry friend, he seemed to be at a loss for words (not very common for a pastor, right?).

When he found the right words, this pastor described why his fast-growing, 7,000-member church is missing the point. To the community, this church appears muscular and fit on the outside. But inside, he described the mono-generational make-up of the congregation as if it were a disease.

HOW CAN THE CHURCH BE THE CHURCH WHEN SO MANY MEMBERS OF THE BODY ARE MISSING?

They're busting at the seams with creative twenty-somethings who are willing to play in the band or volunteer with the middle school students. But the seasoned sages who have walked the journey a little longer are nowhere to be found. At thirty-five years of age, the lead pastor is considered one of the older adults at the church.

Of course, the idea of changing anything at this particular church seems outrageous to its members, because their church is growing like wildfire. Yet this pastor senses that the long-term discipleship of both young and old is at risk.

Now hear us clearly: *We would never suggest this church should just close its doors and disband on the basis of its age demographic.* If that were the case, many churches across North America should be closing simply because most of their members are over age fifty-five. But this case study highlights a common question felt at both ends of that spectrum: **How can the church be the church when so many members of the body are missing?** Can it be that we're actually missing out on something important by staying in our age-segregated communities? If so, what can we do about it?

MULTIGENERATIONAL VS. INTERGENERATIONAL

Even if your church feels more "in the middle" on this one—you can look around and see eight- to twenty-eight- to eighty-eight-year-olds—from our experience even *multigenerational* churches have a hard time being truly *intergenerational*. In other words, multiple generations may be represented, but the connections between those groups are often weak—perhaps even when they worship together on a regular basis.

Put another way, if a fifteen-year old grabs a hamburger at a church barbecue and then sits alone among hundreds of senior citizens, she would be participating in a *multigenerational* event. Now if that same girl was invited by an eighty-year-old lady to join her for dinner and share stories, the two might share a fruitful *intergenerational* experience. Hamburgers aside, when you look around your church and the way it functions, do you see more examples of the former or the latter kind of interaction?

ALL OF US, ALL IN

Simply put, we're convinced that **the whole church needs the whole church.** What many churches find so exciting about implementing Sticky Faith is that it requires *all of us,* and it invites us to be *all-in* as part of the faith family.

When we talk to groups of grandparents, their eyes glimmer as we highlight their importance in young people's lives. They long to be told that they still have something significant to contribute (besides their money) to the church.

Senior adults also have something to learn. Older folks need younger people in their lives in order to grow in their faith too.

Just last week we heard from a seventy-five-year-old man who is a Sunday morning table leader for seventh and eighth grade boys in his church. When asked why he loves this ministry, he said that folks his age no longer talk about changing the world. They've often settled for an "it is what it is" perspective. Not so with seventh and eighth graders. They're still curious about everything, and they see life as an adventure. This man is *gaining life and faith* through the unrestricted energy of teenage boys. In God's economy, they need him and he needs them.

This Sticky Faith interdependence resonates with the Apostle Paul's analogy of the body. In order for the entire body to be healthy, each part must perform its necessary function (see Romans 12, 1 Corinthians 12, and Ephesians 4 for three recurrences of this image). When any part is missing or excluded, the body is not complete.

YOUTH MINISTRY   CHILDREN'S MINISTRY   SENIOR ADULTS   SMALL GROUPS   MISSIONS

BEYOND SILOS

In working with leaders all across North America, we've yet to meet a church that *intentionally* built ministry silos to separate groups within their congregation. Yet we've met hundreds of leaders who find themselves trapped inside of unintentionally created silos.

What is a ministry silo? Simply put, a silo is a department or ministry in a church that functions autonomously from the other ministries. One of our cohort churches actually names these entities "divisions," which paints a clear word picture for what happens among the body. Churches that are deeply entrenched in silos experience uncomfortable competition, lack of awareness of one another, and a type of territorialism that can get pretty ugly.

One of the ways silos harm churches is by preventing a unified ministry vision. If all the people in a church rowboat are not communicating, they're rowing in different directions. The boat simply spins. The harder each person paddles, the faster the boat spins 'round and 'round.

In order to stop the spinning experienced by many congregations, we must pause and lay down the paddles. Here are a few suggestions from the experiences of churches in our cohorts who have rowed together toward more intergenerational ministry:

GET IN THE SAME ROOM

If your church wants to get out of ministry silos, you'll have to carve out regular time for a cross section of all ministries to gather for the sole purpose of creating a stickier ethos in your congregation. Each time you gather, share signs of hope you're seeing around the community, tell stories of future hope, and dream up ways to create intergenerational experiences.

REVISIT YOUR ROLES

Regardless of church size, gather the entire team of ministry-specific leaders in the same room to look at job descriptions. If you're mostly volunteer-run, work up role descriptions that include the responsibilities of those volunteers. Talk together about what it would look like to tweak your roles in ways that might increase interaction among ministry areas.

CONSIDER SOME RESTRUCTURING

Many Sticky Faith churches have completely restructured their staff organizational charts to reduce siloization. Sometimes the first and greatest step to unify churches is to dissolve the walls between children's and youth ministries. Being willing to talk openly about these tensions can at least jump-start the conversation.

CULTIVATE A NEW LANGUAGE

If we speak in terms of "us and them," we will wind up with a church full of "us and thems." Rethink how you speak of each generation and how you title generational ministries in your church. It might be that teenagers don't like to be called kids, and senior adults are not so fond of being called old. One ministry to older adults we know of actually bans the use of "senior" in favor of the word "mature." That might not seem to matter if you're under seventy, but take a moment to ask someone on the other side of that line for their perspective.

A great place to start learning is to return to *listening* (see Module 1, Part 5). How does each generation refer to themselves? What are some of the values that each generation is excited to talk about? Listening is not simply the first step in implementing Sticky Faith; it is necessary at *every step* of the process.

Part 2

HOW FAST CAN I MAKE CHANGES?

▶ **VIDEO**

Download the five-minute video "How Fast Can I Make Changes?" from stickyfaithlaunchkit.org and consider using it with your Launch Team to start a conversation about the pace of change. Be sure to listen for Kara's story about our youth pastor friend Keegan at the three-minute mark.

Great ideas demand immediate and big action, right? Sometimes, but not always.

Many of us who become inspired by Sticky Faith want to let everyone know and then try to make a lot of change quickly. After all, we can see clearly where we want to head, and we think our role as leaders is to take people to that destination.

The problem with this approach is that it ratchets up the pressure for the change to succeed right away, and it doesn't provide any freedom to fail or to learn from mistakes. That's why we have to be wise in the pace and scope of the changes we launch.

EXPERIMENT ON THE MARGINS

Instead of the jump-first approach, consider creating *experiments on the margins*.

Don't make a big announcement. Don't cancel all of your regular programming.

Instead, design small experiments and invite a few others into those experiments. If they flop, you have the opportunity to learn from your mistakes ... *and hardly anyone will know.*

For example, gather a group of both adults and teenagers to work together on a creative arts project at a local family shelter one Saturday. Chances are good that you'll learn a lot from that experiment that will lay the groundwork for the next one. And then when you're ready to talk more openly to the whole congregation about intergenerational initiatives, you will already have stories in your back pocket. This approach protects you from making a big announcement too soon and then failing publicly in ways that actually slow down or even cripple your progress.

Many leaders have told us that simply using the word "experiment" releases a lot of tension and relaxes expectations. Call it an experiment, give it a clear timeline, and launch away knowing that whether you succeed or fail, you'll learn and grow.

The problem is not that failure is bad. We actually can learn quite a bit from failure. But congregations sometimes dish out high penalties for failure, especially failures that involve attendance or finances. So rather than start your intergenerational ministry plan by dissolving Sunday morning programming and dropping teenagers back into "big church" worship every week, you might want to look for incremental steps that lead toward bigger shifts at a rate your community can handle.

THE PROBLEM IS NOT THAT FAILURE IS BAD. WE ACTUALLY CAN LEARN QUITE A BIT FROM FAILURE.

▶ VIDEO

Is it ever appropriate to experiment out in the open with big changes? Watch the one-minute video "Can I Experiment Publicly with Change?" to learn more from Dr. Scott Cormode. Download it at stickyfaithlaunchkit.org.

▶ ADDITIONAL RESOURCES

Want to explore the pace of change a bit further? We've listed some helpful links for you at stickyfaithlaunchkit.org.

WHAT NOW?

Start looking for ways to experiment on the margins. Module 4, Part 3 below dives into all kinds of practical ideas and tips. Before you head there, begin by leading this exercise with your Launch Team:

REVIEW

Look back at your Breakthrough Plan (See Module 1, Part 8) and the core change areas you've identified, along with the specific goals and plans you've created.

ASSESS

Based on what you've written already and what you know about your congregation, how does the pace of change feel? Is it about right, too fast, or too slow? Do any particular changes feel like experiments on the margins? Do any feel like major shifts for your church?

IDENTIFY

Identify one or two first experiments on the margins that could take you forward in your Breakthrough Plan without risking too much public failure too soon.

PLAN

Make concrete plans to try these experiments!

SCHEDULE

Set dates to come back together as a team and debrief each experiment. Be sure to put these follow-up meetings on the calendar as soon as you plan an experiment, so they're not forgotten. Use the questions below to reflect on each experiment:

> » What went well?
> » What didn't go so well?
> » What can we learn?
> » If an experiment flopped, are there some elements that did go well that we'd like to continue? How could we modify this experiment and try something different?
> » What did we learn from this experiment about introducing change in our congregation?
> » Now that we've experimented in this way, where do we go next? What's the best next step to introduce the change we hope to see?

Part 3

TIPS, TOOLS, AND EXPERIMENTS IN INTER-GENERATIONAL MINISTRY

LAUNCH TIP

"Every June we plan a worship service that highlights the promotion of our kindergarten students, sixth grade students, and high school seniors. We intentionally plan every element of this service to speak about and illustrate our vision for being a Sticky Faith Church. We use a narrative written by one of our volunteers that weaves together each element. Each age level leader honors every student and recognizes their uniqueness and gifting.

This service has two goals: to help our young people see themselves as a valuable part of the church, and to help our church body embrace and understand their role in the discipleship of young people. Looking at kindergarten students who will be sixth graders in six years, and sixth graders who will be graduating from high school in six years, is a powerful tangible illustration of the role of the church across the seasons of childhood and adolescence."

NATE ROSKAM
COMMUNITY LIFE PASTOR
Nampa First Nazarene, Nampa, Idaho

Imagine your ideal neighborhood—not only the street layout and building architecture, but also the relationships. How would the neighbors interact with each other? What would friendships look like? How would neighborhood barbeques or block parties feel? How often would neighbors interact outside, enter each other's homes, borrow and lend stuff, and carpool to work or school?

Imagine the intergenerational relationships in that neighborhood. Perhaps a teenager walks down the street to teach basic cell phone skills to a seventy-five-year-old, while a retired schoolteacher is tutoring the fourth grader next door in math.

Two threads that weave through this neighborhood scenario are *physical proximity* and *diversity of age*. Intergenerational relationships require both elements, whether in a neighborhood or a church. Different generations have to actually exist and to exist close enough to one another to rub shoulders and spark conversations.

WHILE SOME
CHURCHES MAY
APPEAR TO
HAVE A GREAT
INTERGENERATIONAL
LIFE TOGETHER, OUR
EXPERIENCE IS THAT
MOST CHURCHES
HAVE TO WORK AT IT.

While some churches may appear to have a great intergenerational life together, our experience is that *most churches have to work at it*. Most likely your church is generationally lopsided in some way, perhaps missing one generation and overcrowded by another. Or maybe every generation is present, but it's as if you're living in different neighborhoods across town. The goal isn't a perfect balance, but rather a move toward healthy representation and interaction.

Think of a ladder that is missing a few rungs here and there. Traveling up and down is not only diffi-

THINK OF A LADDER THAT IS MISSING A FEW RUNGS HERE AND THERE. TRAVELING UP AND DOWN IS NOT ONLY DIFFICULT, BUT IT ACTUALLY MIGHT BE IMPOSSIBLE.

cult, but it actually might be impossible. In a similar way, the local church will struggle to share the stories and wisdom from generation to generation if entire age groups are missing or inactive. These next reminders will help you work toward getting more rungs on the ladder.

YOU THINK ABOUT THIS MORE THAN THEY DO

Remember that you are likely out in front of the rest of your church in dreaming about Sticky Faith. Make sure that terms like "Sticky Faith" and "intergenerational ministry" are explained and supported by stories. Lead with statements like, *"You may have heard this before, but I want to remind all of us again of what we mean by intergenerational ministry and why it is important in our church."* In many ways, implementing Sticky Faith will require one foot on the gas and one foot on the brake as you educate and re-educate your congregation.

 SOME FOLKS IN YOUR CHURCH WILL HEAR ABOUT STICKY FAITH AND COME OUT OF THE GATES IN A DEAD SPRINT

Despite what we just said, be prepared to deal with propositions like, "I'm on board! Give me a kid to mentor." These are exciting responses, but a church with no system to help plug people in or take natural next steps will get caught on their heels. For example, before inspiring your church with a Sticky-Faith-focused sermon, make a list of ways adults could get involved with young people. Include opportunities for low-, medium-, and high-level commitments, and write short job descriptions for specific ministry needs. The beauty of this approach is that you'll have an answer for those who are excited to jump in and serve. They can see all of the opportunities and begin to discern where they best fit. Think about how to tap into a wide variety of talents and skills in your congregation.

Always start by helping adults think of natural relationships that already exist. You may not want to become the friendship matchmaker for your entire church. When someone is ready to be "sticky," you can ask them to start by thinking about neighbors, nieces and nephews, and other relationships that already exist within the congregation. Parents, other adults, students, and ministry volunteers should all play roles in creating webs of relationships. If you start in the middle of everything, you will stay in the middle of everything. So when that excited grandpa approaches you with his great idea you can respond by asking, "Who are three younger people you already interact with at least every other week or so?" We have found that potential intergenerational relationships are often closer than we imagine.

 ▶ **INSTRUCTIONAL NOTE**

Often when we begin to talk about creating relationships between young people and adults, we get asked about safety. Our best suggestion is to work within any safety systems you already have in place for background screenings and precautions before creating situations where adults and kids might be together beyond large-group gatherings. If you don't have a system in place, consult your church leadership, denominational offices, or research church and nonprofit child safety standards online.

YOU'RE TALKING ABOUT A GAME CHANGER

When you talk about intergenerational relationships, you're asking your congregation to think less in terms of youth ministry volunteers or "chaperones," and more in terms of creating a sticky web of relationships around each young person.

When you take middle schoolers to the amusement park, you want one chaperone for every five kids to make sure Luis doesn't get brain trauma from riding the head-smashing roller coaster fifteen consecutive times. In other words, this ratio is often about defense and prevention. Encouraging your congregation to flip the ratio to 5:1 means you're hoping that five influential adults will invest in the life of every young person who walks through the doors of the church. Shifting from 1:5 to 5:1 is a game changer.

The 5:1 ratio is more about offense than defense. We realize the entire church is needed and must be mobilized in the long-term discipleship of teenagers. Parents, youth volunteers, and students themselves get to participate in creating this sticky web of faith. One leader told us how offended she was the first time a student introduced his small group leader as his "youth pastor." At the time, she couldn't believe she was snubbed for a volunteer. Now she actually encourages her students to see these significant adults as *"youth pastors."* Another Sticky Faith church calls ALL of their children's and youth ministry volunteers "pastors" in order to value the role of each adult in the life of a young person.

YOU CAN'T DO THIS WITHOUT THE INFLUENCERS

In order to launch Sticky Faith effectively, you'll want to generate curiosity and enthusiasm among the whole congregation. This means vision and encouragement about Sticky Faith must come not only from the middle of the organization (where you likely live as a youth leader) but also from the top. The senior pastor, key lay leaders, and other significant influencers all play critical roles in your implementation strategy. Below in Module 4, Part 4, we give more tips for talking with and understanding senior leaders. Now is the time to begin making a list of which people hold the most influence in various pockets of your congregation, and start scheduling meetings with those folks over coffee or lunch to share the Sticky Faith vision one on one.

MOST CONGREGATIONS ARE ALREADY CONVINCED THAT YOUNG PEOPLE ARE WALKING AWAY FROM THE CHURCH, AND THEY'RE AFRAID OF WHAT THIS MEANS FOR THE FUTURE OF THEIR KIDS AND GRANDKIDS, AS WELL AS THE CHURCH AS A WHOLE.

A TOUR THAT HELPS YOUR CHURCH GET ON BOARD

When you were younger, maybe you had the experience of going door to door selling some kind of candy or wrapping paper so you could raise money for your soccer team or marching band. You didn't really care about the product very much, if at all. It's hard to sell what you don't believe in.

Now imagine going "door to door" throughout your congregation proclaiming Sticky Faith to various groups. You believe in it, you're passionate about it, and the good news is, it's often an "easy sell" to cast the vision. Sticky Faith research is usually believable once it's clearly shared. Most congregations are already convinced that young people are walking away from the church, and they're afraid of what this means for the future of their kids and grandkids, as well as the church as a whole.

PLANNING YOUR TOUR

Start by making a list of all the pockets of people who gather in your church. Think about the "mature women's" knitting group, the MOPS (mothers of preschoolers), discipleship-based small groups, adult Sunday school classes, your primary leadership group (depending on your tradition, this could be an elder board, church council, or some other designation), the singles ministry, and beyond. Once you create a comprehensive list, run it by your Launch Team for input on who might be missing and which groups would be the easiest places to start. Then design a church-wide tour in three different phases:

TOUR 1

Make a first trip to each group for the purpose of framing the problem, introducing the research, sharing your ideas about solutions, and letting them respond. Be sure to have some tangible next steps that you'd like folks to make. End each leg of this tour by saying, "I'll be back."

TOUR 2

Take another tour to the same groups three to six months later. Go back and ask what they heard you emphasize the first time. This is your chance to see what resonates with your congregation. Tell some more stories to clarify the vision. Then ask what kinds of conversations and action grew out of their particular group. Ask how they have witnessed sticky relationships in the church since the last time you visited.

TOUR 3

This is the vision recasting tour. After about a year, swing through your groups again to check in, cast vision, and tell story after story of life change witnessed in the congregation in the last twelve months. Be prepared to really listen well on this tour, as it may come right about the time folks start to get concerned about some of the changes they're noticing. This is a good window to assess how the pace of change feels to various subgroups.

WHAT TO SAY ON THE TOUR

START WITH THEIR STORIES

Before you make bold statements, start by asking some questions. In groups of three or four, have them respond to these two questions:

> » Who influenced you in your faith when you were younger? What do you most remember about them?
> » Share one practical way you personally could influence a younger person in the faith.

Allow the groups to discuss this for a little while. It is amazing what the power of memory can do when people recall these influences. Then invite a few moments of sharing with the larger group, asking what themes stand out to people from the stories that were shared. Be careful to limit this to sharing themes rather than whole stories, and watch your time so you don't get sidetracked from the content you're setting up. When a good transition theme is mentioned, connect it with Sticky Faith and launch into your presentation.

USE IMAGES AND STORIES TO SHARE ABOUT STICKY FAITH

By now you might be good at this when it comes to your Launch Team, volunteers, or even parents (loop back to Modules 2 and 3 for more ideas and resources). But you might want to narrow this down to a few core images as you go on tour. After all, chances are you'll only get thirty to forty-five minutes with each group (or perhaps sixty if they really like you). Consider ahead of time which main points and images most resonate with your particular congregation and which stories of future hope might get a positive response.

Here are a few examples of images (you can also make up your own) that might help you communicate about Sticky Faith and in particular about intergenerational ministry. As you go from group to group, consider enhancing your words with props or slides. You may want to save some illustrations or videos for subsequent tours or other contexts. For example, we've used the adoption video referenced on page 211 in sermons for a very powerful image of what the church can become.

HERE ARE A FEW EXAMPLES OF IMAGES (YOU CAN ALSO MAKE UP YOUR OWN) THAT MIGHT HELP YOU COMMUNICATE ABOUT STICKY FAITH AND IN PARTICULAR ABOUT INTERGENERATIONAL MINISTRY.

THE KIDS' TABLE

THE BATON

THE TO-DO LIST

ADOPTION

TRUE STORIES OF INTERGENERATIONAL RELATIONSHIPS

THE KIDS' TABLE

This analogy highlights the problem of segregating young people from adults. For added effect you can set up a demonstration of two separate tables each time you present Sticky Faith, or you can show the "Tale of Two Tables" video. If you don't have much time or space is limited, a simple picture of a kids' table at a family gathering can also frame this well.

 ▶ VIDEO

Download the "Tale of Two Tables" video at stickyfaithlaunchkit.org.

THE BATON

Find a baton that is used in relay races, or just make your own out of a paper towel roll. Use the baton as a symbol of the transition from high school into college, the military, or the workforce. As you are explaining the importance of transitions, drop the baton on the floor to symbolize what happens to many of the students in our youth ministries as they take the next step. The church tends to drop them once they graduate from high school ministry, and young people tend to drop their faith. Share a story of a student who was "dropped" and then ask the group to think about ways we can stop the baton dropping.

THE TO-DO LIST

Ask groups to help you write out a list of what Christians "do" and "don't do." Get them started if needed with examples like: don't cuss, go to church, don't have sex before you get married, bring your Bible to church, etc. Share that we often unintentionally reduce the gospel of Jesus Christ to a list like this. The result is that our teenagers believe God likes them if they follow the list, and God wants nothing to do with them when they break the rules. This is what Dallas Willard calls the "gospel of sin management."[1] Ask for ideas about how we can all model a life of faith for young people that points to the true gospel of grace and reconciliation.

ADOPTION

One of the vivid images we use to describe the way the church can embrace young people is adoption. Just as God adopts us into his family (see Galatians, especially 4:7; Ephesians 2:19-20; and Romans 8:14-17), the congregation is called to adopt young people into the church family. If you can capture it ahead of time or use Internet access on your tour, consider sharing this powerful three-minute video of a family adoption from the television series *Parenthood*.

1   See Dallas Willard, *The Divine Conspiracy: Rediscovering Our Hidden Life in God*, (New York: HarperOne, 1998).

▶ VIDEO
At the time of publication this clip could be found on YouTube on NBC's channel under the title "Victor Becomes a Braverman – Parenthood" at http://www.youtube.com/watch?v=B0N8P2JMbeo (uploaded January 22, 2013).

After you show the video, ask for observations about how this could be a picture of the church. Then share that while this scene is full of messy family relationships and an adolescent who seems captivated by the promise of a visit to the vending machine, the power of adoption clearly changes everyone involved.

TRUE STORIES OF INTERGENERATIONAL RELATIONSHIPS

Images and Hollywood renditions are great, but there's nothing like a true story to inspire change. If you can share stories from your own congregation, please do so (though you should ask for permission from those involved). You could also consider showing one of these two videos as examples of how Sticky Faith has played out in other churches where older adults and teenagers found unlikely connections.

 ▶ VIDEO
SUE & NICK
Found at stickyfaithlaunchkit.org

 ▶ VIDEO
JONAH & BOB
Found at stickyfaithlaunchkit.org

 3 SHARE YOUR DREAM, AND GIVE THEM A NEXT STEP
As we shared in Module 1, Part 9, youth pastor Nate Stratman went on tour in his church sharing "a stat, a story, and a dream." The dream is where you clearly lay out your hope for the congregation. You might share an idea from your Breakthrough Plan, but you might not want to go into that much detail at this point. Come prepared with a set of possible action steps that a class or an individual could take in response. Close in prayer, and be sure to tell them you'll be back again in a few months.

LAUNCH TIP

"In an attempt to make intergenerational ministry a part of our congregational culture, we experimented last summer by changing up our Sunday morning programming for a couple of months. Children and student ministries met during our first worship service, and parents were encouraged to find ways to serve. Then we asked everyone to stay and to worship as families during the second hour.

To be more inclusive with our children and students, we also handed out a worksheet for kids that had fill-in-the-blank spaces from the sermon and other activities that were connected to the theme. For completing the handout, kids would get candy at the end of the service (yeah, we know that's kind of like bribery). The teaching pastor each week worked hard to speak directly to kids and teenagers throughout the service, addressing them specifically and applying the teaching to their lives.

Here's what we learned from our experiment:

1. Candy is a powerful motivator. Kids did the sheet. Kids connected (even if superficially) with the pastor. But more than that, they were often engaged. On a few occasions when the teaching pastor asked a rhetorical question during the sermon, a child or teenager answered out loud.

2. This experiment created some lopsided attendance. Our second service was often packed, while the first service was much emptier. That also made it challenging to recruit volunteers during our second service since many of our families were attending the service together.

3. Including everyone required some adaptation. More kids in the service made it noisier and disruptive at times. We learned that we needed to work harder to make the worship music inclusive by adding a song or two that kids recognize and feel more comfortable singing.

4. Lastly, we learned that no matter how hard you try, some people won't buy in to what you think are great ideas. We did have at least two families this summer tell us they are looking for another church because they did not like our experiment.

Overall, we counted our experiment a huge success. We had great pastoral support, and we tried to tell a lot of stories to share our vision. Twice during the summer, families shared during worship about their own successes, failures, and thoughts on worshiping as a family. Every week kids were addressed in some way during the service, and regularly throughout the summer they were told they are a valuable and necessary part of our congregation.

This fall we're back to offering children's and youth ministry during both services. But it's only a temporary return to 'normal.' We're already planning our next experiment."

KRIS FERNHOUT
STUDENT MINISTRY PASTOR
Christ Community Church Olathe Campus, Olathe, Kansas

EXPERIMENTS FROM STICKY FAITH CHURCHES

Need ideas for what kinds of experiments might work to connect young and old? Below you'll find a handful of ideas from churches we've worked with in our Sticky Faith Cohorts.

INTERGENERATIONAL WORSHIP

This has probably been the most tried and most diverse context for creating intergenerational relationships. Our biggest advice here is to make any experiment as contextual as possible. If adults and kids never worship together in your context, start small. Invite kids to join the first fifteen minutes of the service, or worship together once a quarter. When you do, consider what hospitality to young people looks like in the context of a shared worship environment. Further, while many churches hold an annual "Youth Sunday," consider how even this day could become more intergenerational, rather than simply switching roles for one Sunday. Another idea is to create a sign-up system so every greeter, singer, announcement giver, and prayer leader has a younger partner/apprentice each week. You may be surprised at the relationships that naturally take off when different generations are given the chance to serve together in worship.

MIXED MISSIONS

Serving together beyond the church can be an incredible catalyst for intergenerational relationships. Whether these are weekly experiences in your community or short-term mission trips out of the country, here are a few helpful tips from experienced leaders:

SPREAD OUT JOBS EVENLY

Your mission trip may set up a teenager to lead the morning devotions while a middle-aged CEO is placed in charge of filling water coolers for the day. This can be fruitful for both of them.

BE INTENTIONAL WITH PAIRING

If someone is skilled and another person wants to learn that particular skill, make sure to pair them together. The motivation to learn can help relationships grow.

SHARE AND SPECULATE

During a debrief or reflection time, invite the older generation to share about a meaningful experience they had when they were younger. Then let the younger participants speculate what they want to be like when they are older.

UNIVERSAL LOVE LANGUAGES

Without fail, food and fun can bring a wide range of people together. We know of one church that held a pie contest where most of the bakers were older and all of the judges were younger. After the contest, all ages sat around eating pie together, followed by activities that were specifically set up to appeal to many interests. Young and old played board games, learned to paint pots and plant mini herb gardens in them, or strummed guitars and sang together. This is neither rocket science nor flashy ministry! It's simply setting up a fun venue in which people can experience time and space with one another while making memories.

THE BABYSITTING BOOK

Families with younger kids are often looking for babysitters. Unfortunately, many of these families have little interaction with older teenagers. Host a Red Cross training event at your church for teenagers who want to be "officially trained" as babysitters. Then put together a manual with all of the students' names, where they live, whether they can drive or not, as well some information about their interests and hobbies. Clearly communicate a hope that this ministry goes both ways. Encourage families to invest in that babysitter not only financially, but also relationally. We know several families who make it a point to come home after their date night to spend thirty minutes hanging out with the babysitter (and paying them for that time as well). These opportunities can lead to great relationships.

SENIOR TO SENIOR

A number of churches have begun some sort of ministry linking senior adults with senior high students (or specifically twelfth-grade seniors). In one congregation, each student is adopted by a senior adult at the start of the year. The pairs are encouraged to meet once a month to share life over coffee or a game. In a few cases, students who haven't really connected with the youth ministry very well have found these relationships to be significant connecting points to the church family.

▶ ADDITIONAL RESOURCES
NEED MORE IDEAS?

We've cultivated a whole crop of stories and ideas you can harvest on our website. See stickyfaith.org/stories or search the site for specific keywords (e.g., intergenerational, mentoring, mission trips). Submit a story of your own using our Sticky Faith Stories form! We'd love to hear how your church is experimenting.

Part 4

HOW CAN I HELP MY SENIOR PASTOR UNDERSTAND WHAT NEEDS TO CHANGE?

 # LAUNCH TIP

"I was told the process would be slow, and this has been so true. When I get excited about something, I want to do it all right now. Knowing in advance this was going to be slow has been a gift. I had heard it might take two or three years for our staff to buy into intergenerational ministry, and another three to five years for full implementation in the church. My experience affirms this.

I am a little bit relieved to know the process is slow, because it means I can take it at a healthy pace. It turns out to be good for myself, the staff, and the church. It also means I need to be willing to walk through this journey with my congregation and our leadership, not just sprint ahead and get frustrated with everyone else."

KEEGAN LENKER
PASTOR OF INTERGENERATIONAL DISCIPLESHIP
Pasadena Nazarene, Pasadena, California

"The glass ceiling."

It's a phrase generally used to describe how specific groups (typically women or certain ethnicities) can advance only so far before they hit a wall. Your church probably has its own glass ceilings. One of those might be a limit to your level of influence.

Since Sticky Faith affects your entire congregation, you'll need your senior leadership fully invested in order to see much systemic change. In other words, you need to lead up.

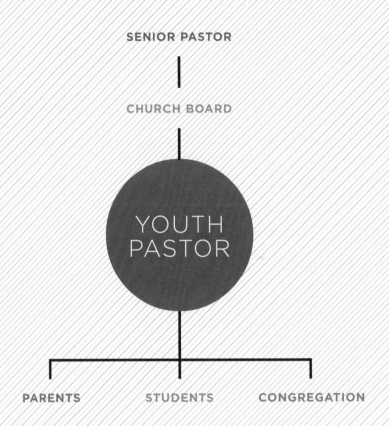

In your relationship with your senior pastor in particular, you're in an awkward position of wanting to lead your church forward in Sticky Faith initiatives while not having the power to make ultimate decisions or perhaps even to influence the entire congregation. "Leading up" means that you leverage your hard work in this launch process and find skillful ways to influence senior leaders toward both *understanding* and *action*.

▶ **VIDEO**
Download the three-minute video "How Can I Help My Senior Pastor Understand That Something Needs to Change?" from stickyfaithlaunchkit.org.

YOUTH WORKERS TEND TO MAKE TWO MISTAKES IN LEADING UP

1 The first mistake is describing the changes we'd like to see as if they're brand new and our church has never experienced them. The reality is that the threads of the changes we want to bring about are likely already woven throughout our church's history. As you meet with your Launch Team, brainstorm together ways your future vision connects with the past tradition of your community. One church that had been burned to the ground by fire twenty years ago captured that image to link their vision with the past. The older members of the congregation remembered well the ways the community came together, working to rebuild in the midst of the ashes. Pointing to the fire-marked stained glass windows, the youth pastor was able to remind the leadership that those marks capture memories of the church surrounding one another with support.

2 The second mistake is to describe the changes we want to see in terms that are meaningful to *us*. Of course Sticky Faith resonates with us; we work with teenagers all the time. However, we need to convince our senior leadership that these changes are important to the whole church. In order to do so, we need to think through what is going be meaningful to *them*. What are your senior pastor's love languages or favorite emphases when talking about the church? What's already important to the DNA of your congregation? Does the change need to be grounded in scripture? Or is it important that it will ultimately bring more people to the church? When you share about the changes you want to see happen, make sure to use terms that communicate well to your senior leaders. You don't need to do this in a manipulative or deceptive way, but tailoring your language and angling your message shows that you're paying attention and that you care about what your leadership cares about.

This is also where you can bring out the napkin and pencil over a cup of coffee. Begin by drawing the problem that half of teenagers from youth groups like yours will drift from the church and from God (See Module 1, Part 3 for ideas on how to illustrate these points quickly).

At this point, ask your senior leaders how they respond to that statistic. What do they see as they look at the church? Hopefully they will ask something like, "Why do *you* think this is happening?" Your response can reflect more of the Sticky Faith research by explaining three major shifts from:

A BEHAVIOR-BASED GOSPEL TO A GRACE-BASED GOSPEL

A TWO-TABLE CHURCH TO WELCOMING YOUNG PEOPLE AROUND ONE FAMILY TABLE

"DRY-CLEANER" PARENTING TO MINISTRY PARTNERSHIP

As you have explained the problem and the responses using your napkin, now allow those leaders to do some dreaming of their own. Ask for their ideas to implement Sticky Faith in your context. Ask for permission to share some of the ideas you've been working on with the Launch Team. Invite your pastor's support, and ask what more he or she might need in order to learn more about the vision and be able to offer the support you're asking for. Close by asking your senior leaders how you can better support and pray for them.

WATCH OUT FOR COMPETING COMMITMENTS

▶ **VIDEO**

"Why Is My Pastor First Open to Ideas, but Later Resists Change?" Watch this two-and-a-half-minute video from stickyfaithlaunchkit.org to understand why this dilemma often feels like a roadblock but doesn't have to be.

After that first meeting, you might feel like you've done your job when it comes to your pastor's support of your new Sticky Faith ideas. That may not exactly be the case. Down the road a few weeks or months, you might approach your leadership for further support in some aspect of your plan and suddenly feel like you've hit a wall.

What happened?

What we need to understand is that each of us, including pastors, experience *competing commitments*. At the same time that you go to your pastor to request changes and he or she says yes, the worship pastor might approach the pastor with another set of changes, like improving the quality of the worship service in a way that caters more to older generations than to younger folks. If one of your suggested changes is to bring more children and teenagers into the worship service, the pastor may be faced with two competing commitments. What should you do in this situation?

If you wanted to help your pastor say yes to your request, you would need to anticipate that this might represent a competing commitment. In the example above, you might suggest that there are ways to bring more teenagers into the worship service that wouldn't compromise the quality. Then commit to team with the worship pastor to brainstorm possible solutions rather than putting your senior pastor in a position of playing favorites or choosing between those commitments. You may not know all of the competing commitments your pastor is juggling, but chances are good you know a number of them.

WHAT NOW?

 ▶ **HANDOUT**

COMPETING COMMITMENTS

Available to the right and online at stickyfaithlaunchkit.org.

You will become more effective as a leader in bringing about change if you're able to anticipate potential competing commitments and present solutions up front. The exercise below will help you and your Launch Team do just that. The first column of the chart includes an example of two competing commitments: intergenerational worship and improving the quality of the worship service by targeting a specific demographic. In the empty boxes below, write down other changes you'd like to introduce. Then anticipate the competing commitments your pastor or board might face. In many cases, there may be two, three, or even more competing commitments.

The second column is for you to think through what your proposed change would cost this pastor or board. What would they have to give up in another area to accommodate your change? This is an opportunity for you to think through what is most meaningful to them and the language you might use to communicate in their terms.

The third column is to brainstorm solutions you might offer to resolve the tension between commitments. Be sure to consider again the culture and history of your church, as the changes you're proposing may not be brand new.

CONSIDER THESE QUESTIONS TOGETHER AFTER COMPLETING THE CHART:
  » What is important to our senior pastor or church board? How can we communicate our proposed changes in ways that are meaningful to them?
  » Are the changes we're proposing brand new? Are there elements of the changes that are already present in our church's culture or history?
  » For the changes where there is not an easy solution, does one side need to win while the other loses, or is there way to make it a win-win?
  » Have we searched our hearts regarding these changes? Is our focus really on what is best for the whole church, or are we focused on what is best for us personally or for the youth ministry?

 ▶ **ADDITIONAL RESOURCES**

For additional resources on leading up, see the links we've provided at stickyfaithlaunchkit.org.

COMPETING COMMITMENTS

COMPETING COMMITMENTS OUR PASTOR OR CHURCH BOARD FACES	WHAT IT WILL COST THE PASTOR OR BOARD TO IMPLEMENT OUR CHANGE	WHAT WE CAN DO TO PROVIDE A SOLUTION
» Bringing more teenagers into the worship service (our proposed change) » Improving the quality of the worship service by tailoring the music to forty- to fifty-year-old adults (the worship pastor's proposed change)	» The worship service would not be tailored to a specific demographic » Some people might leave the church	» Brainstorm ideas with the worship pastor for involving students in music leadership alongside adults, encouraging mentoring relationships and skill training » Utilize students as greeters, readers, and communion servers to help increase the engagement of young people in non-musical ways

PROPOSED CHANGE:

COMPETING COMMITMENT:

PROPOSED CHANGE:

COMPETING COMMITMENT:

Part 5

HOW DO I CHANGE THE WAY PEOPLE THINK ABOUT THE MISSION OF YOUTH MINISTRY?

LAUNCH TIP

"Launching Sticky Faith changed my job—literally. It has broadened my focus from only kids and students to also include families, parents, older members, and several areas of ministry where I was not previously involved."

BILL HASLIM
PASTOR OF INTERGENERATIONAL MINISTRIES
Community Presbyterian Church, Danville, CA

By now Sticky Faith has probably changed how you view the mission of youth ministry. One of the inevitable outcomes of immersing yourself in Sticky Faith for very long is a shifting understanding of youth ministry altogether.

You've probably already started doing things outside of your job description. Sooner or later you'll run up against a critique—or a number of critiques—about how you're leading the ministry. When you do, you're faced with an opportunity to cast vision for a new kind of youth ministry.

Unfortunately, changing the way other people think about the mission of youth ministry can be difficult because it involves changing one of their *mental models*. A mental model is the way a person thinks something should be. For example, when we asked you to think about the ideal neighborhood in Module 4, Part 3 above, several images probably immediately popped into your mind. Whether those images involved large lawns and quiet streets or an apartment building next to a small city park depends a lot on the mental model you've created for neighborhoods.

LAUNCH TIP

"We now look at things through a different lens. Our perspective is not just the immediate need, but one that has longevity in mind. We don't just ask, 'Will this event be successful tonight?' but also, 'Will what we do tonight successfully cultivate faith that will last?' Launching Sticky Faith has changed how we program, how we spend our budget, and what we prioritize."

JOHN ROSENSTEEL
NEXT GEN PASTOR
Blackhawk Church, Madison, Wisconsin

 ▶ **VIDEO**

Watch the seven-minute video "How Do I Change the Way People Think About the Mission of Youth Ministry?" Download it from stickyfaithlaunchkit.org.

In asking people to change their mental model of youth ministry, you're challenging their picture of what youth ministry *should be*. Your congregation carries an imagination for youth ministry based on what's happened in the past at that church, as well as what individual members brought with them from their own teenage experiences in other churches. Most likely they picture youth ministry as a separate entity from the rest of the church. If one major goal of Sticky Faith is to shift toward integrating young people into the life of the congregation, people may think you're doing it wrong or not doing your job at all. Your role is to help them live into a new mental model of youth ministry.

YOUR ROLE IS TO HELP THEM LIVE INTO A NEW MENTAL MODEL OF YOUTH MINISTRY.

Thankfully, we have some great examples of this in scripture. Jesus' ministry was all about changing mental models. Several times in the Sermon on the Mount (Matthew 5-7), Jesus said, "You have heard it said, but I say ..." Jesus addressed an old mental model, and then he introduced a new model.

This also occurred in a conversation between Jesus and his disciples in Mark 8. Jesus began by asking, "Who do people say I am?" (v. 27). He was essentially asking, "What mental model do people use to make sense of me?" The disciples explained that some said he was John the Baptist, others said Elijah, and others called him a prophet. Jesus then asked, "Who do you say I am?" (v. 29).

Peter responded with the confession, "You are the Messiah" (v. 29). The disciples had a different mental model for who Jesus was. He was not just a prophet, but also the *Messiah*. Jesus affirmed this, but then he explained that the Messiah must go on to suffer and die. This didn't fit Peter's mental model of what the Messiah was supposed to be, so he rebuked Jesus! Surely Jesus had it wrong.

Why was it so hard for the disciples to accept Jesus' teaching about a suffering Messiah? They were expecting the Messiah to be a conquering king who would claim victory over the Romans. To give up that mental model was to give up a lot. Clearly it took Peter and the other disciples a long time to understand Jesus' version of Messiah. In fact, they really didn't get it until after his death, resurrection, and ascension.

If it was that hard for Jesus to change people's mental models, it's probably not going to be a breeze for us. It may take a long time, and some people may never quite understand what we're trying to do.

WHAT NOW?

As we shared at the start of this launch process, *leadership begins with listening* (see Module 1, Part 5). When it comes to understanding and changing people's mental models of youth ministry, the first step is to listen for those mental models. They will emerge when people share stories about their own experience of youth ministry. In the following exercise, you're going to listen to several groups of people as they share these stories.

The first group to begin with is your youth ministry volunteer team (or you may only want to do this with your Launch Team first). Whether in a group meeting or one-on-one, ask each person to share two types of stories: a time when a youth ministry fulfilled their hopes and a time when a youth ministry failed their expectations.

After they share these stories, reflect on what this says about each person's mental model of youth ministry. Remember, a mental model is a picture of the way a person thinks something *should be*. The following form might be a helpful guide for your reflection:

 ▶ **HANDOUT**

LISTENING FOR MENTAL MODELS
Available to the right, and also at stickyfaithlaunchkit.org.

After you have gone through this exercise with volunteers, have them go out and ask two to four other people in the congregation to share their own experiences in youth ministry. This activity will be most effective if you get input from a wide variety of people. Ask parents, students in your ministry, other key stakeholders or influencers, and your senior pastor.

Once your volunteers have done this, gather your team again and discuss what these stories reveal about people's mental models of youth ministry in your congregation. Use these questions to process together:

> » Are there trends or commonalities among the mental models of youth ministry held by the people at our church? Do different groups of people have competing models?
> » How are these mental models different from the future we envision for our youth ministry? How are they similar?
> » What are the implications of these mental models for the changes we want to make? Will there be a lot of opposition, or will it be easy?
> » How could we go about shifting these mental models? Who needs to be involved in that process? (Hint: Sharing stories of future hope can be incredibly helpful here. See Module 1, Part 6 for a refresher on how to write new stories that help capture this shift in mental models of youth ministry.)

LISTENING FOR MENTAL MODELS

Hopes that were fulfilled:

Expectations that were failed:

What do these reveal about this person's mental model of youth ministry (the way he or she thinks youth ministry *should be*)?

Part 6

TAKING THE NEXT STEP

LAUNCH TIP

"One thing we learned in the Sticky Faith Cohort was to expect pushback when we introduced more intergenerational ministry within our congregation. As I began those conversations, I was surprised to find I was met with very *little* pushback from staff members and others.

That was two years ago.

Today things are different. I lived under the assumption that once people felt informed and got on board, we would be ready to fly. What I discovered was that many people heard, but few were listening. It was not that people were not excited about what they had heard; it was that a lot of our ministries had been operating in isolation from one another for so long. They did not think this affected them at all, so they continued to work in isolation.

I've realized again how important it is to communicate well among ministry leaders, who in turn communicate clearly to those who serve alongside them ... and then to say it all over again and again."

KEEGAN LENKER
PASTOR OF INTERGENERATIONAL DISCIPLESHIP
Pasadena Nazarene, Pasadena, California

You were born to run.

That proposition may sound a bit far-fetched to you, depending on your physical condition and your perspective on running. Some people only run when chased; others seem to find an unexplainable kind of pleasure in tackling ultramarathons of 100-300 miles.

In *Born to Run*, journalist Christopher McDougall narrates his exhaustive investigation of the science, sport, art, and heart of running.[1] His pursuit of American ultraunners and an elusive Mexican running tribe called the *Tarahumara* led him to conclude that humans are, in fact, born to run. Specifically, we're made for *long-distance* running in a unique way that no other creature can claim.

EVEN WHEN RUNNING IS A SOURCE OF JOY AND FULFILLMENT, THERE ARE THOSE MOMENTS MID-RACE WHEN IT'S SO VERY TEMPTING TO GIVE UP.

The trouble is, most of us don't seem to enjoy running. It feels like work. It hurts. We experience health complications and injuries. We can't seem to find time.

ADD YOUR OWN REASONS HERE.

....

....

....

Even when running is a source of joy and fulfillment, there are those moments mid-race when it's so very tempting to give up. You want to just stop, collapse on the side of the road, and hope the emergency team van will pick you up and haul you to the recovery tent.

We're bringing up running not as a last-ditch attempt to guilt you into getting in better physical shape. That would be an awkward way to finish this Launch Kit. No, we mention running because often leading change feels like an ultramarathon. It's not just a sprint. It's not even a regular 26.2-mile marathon; it's *hundreds* of miles of energy, sweat, an aching body, and the temptation to quit.

---

1   Christopher McDougall, *Born to Run: A Hidden Tribe, Superathletes, and the Greatest Race the World Has Never Seen* (New York: Knopf, 2009).

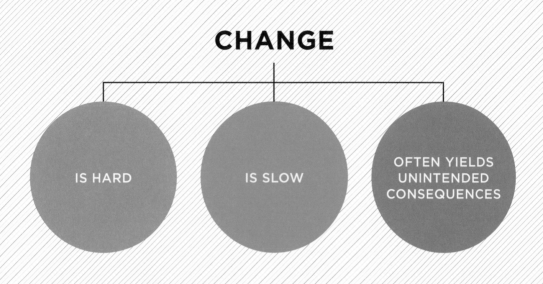

CHANGE

IS HARD

IS SLOW

OFTEN YIELDS UNINTENDED CONSEQUENCES

In the midst of such exhaustion many runners remind themselves: *Just one more step*. One more step gets me further down this road. One more step is better than standing still. One more step keeps me in the race and on my feet.

Throughout this Launch Kit we've mentioned our friend, colleague, and mentor Dr. Scott Cormode a number of times. He's taught us so much about leading change. Yet another one of Scott's catch phrases is "the next faithful step."

 ▶ **ADDITIONAL RESOURCES**
You can access more of Scott's work in person as part of our Sticky Faith Cohorts (see stickyfaith.org/cohort), through his resources at leadership.fuller. edu, or in his book *Making Spiritual Sense: Christian Leaders as Spiritual Interpreters* (Nashville: Abingdon Press, 2006).

Your focus should be on the *next* faithful step. What is the next step right in front of you that will take you one small movement closer to your vision? As leaders we can't force those in our ministries to take the next ten or even five steps all at once. We can't do that ourselves.

We must pace ourselves—and the people we lead—at a rate that is manageable. Like running a distance race, the next step matters just as much as the first—or the last. Every step has its place.

Often once someone has taken the next step, the step after that becomes more bearable. Our imaginations open up to the possibility of a new future. Our "Couch to 5k" program shakes up our norm, and suddenly we're eyeing that upcoming 10k race. We can lead in a way that gently helps those around us see the next faithful step, take it, celebrate it, and learn from it.

You've been deluged with ideas in this Launch Kit. We've tried hard to pack in as much practical advice and as many implementation tools as possible. As we wrap up, we want to encourage you to prayerfully consider the steps you're taking as a leader.

Do the people around you feel encouraged or stomped down? Paced with or left in the dust?

How does your own heart feel? Is there still joy in this race, or did you leave that behind at the last mile marker?

If you're struggling to remember why you started racing in the first place, what would it take to rediscover your passion and joy for ministry with young people? Take a few moments to consider what launched you into ministry. Then make space in your life this week to rekindle that joy again.

Perhaps these words from the author of Hebrews will encourage your steps on this journey:

THEREFORE, SINCE WE ARE SURROUNDED BY SUCH A GREAT CLOUD OF WITNESSES, LET US THROW OFF EVERYTHING THAT HINDERS AND THE SIN THAT SO EASILY ENTANGLES. AND LET US RUN WITH PERSEVERANCE THE RACE MARKED OUT FOR US, FIXING OUR EYES ON JESUS, THE PIONEER AND PERFECTER OF FAITH. FOR THE JOY SET BEFORE HIM HE ENDURED THE CROSS, SCORNING ITS SHAME, AND SAT DOWN AT THE RIGHT HAND OF THE THRONE OF GOD. CONSIDER HIM WHO ENDURED SUCH OPPOSITION FROM SINNERS, SO THAT YOU WILL NOT GROW WEARY AND LOSE HEART.

HEBREWS 12:1-3

You are not alone as you run. Not only did Jesus go before you, but you are also surrounded by a great cloud of witnesses that cheer along the roadside as you go. And when it comes down to it, it's Jesus who authors and perfects faith; he's the one who starts and completes faith for us and for the young people we serve. Sticky Faith, in the end, isn't our work—it's God's. So as you continue taking faithful step after faithful step, may you lean into the one who is faithful to us all.

WHAT NOW?

 ▶ **ADDITIONAL RESOURCES**

As we noted in Module 1, Part 5, we've created an online survey to help you—and us—measure the effectiveness of your ministry in various Sticky Faith areas both before and after your launch process. Take a few moments to complete that survey now at stickyfaithlaunchkit.org to track your growth in these areas over the course of this launch process.

Earlier we suggested that we can lead in a way that gently helps those around us *see* the next faithful step, *take* it, *celebrate* it, and *learn from* it. Let's break those down into practical movements:

SEE THE NEXT FAITHFUL STEP

» Consider the running metaphor in this section in light of your own ministry pace. Imagine pulling yourself to the side of the road to check your vital signs. What do you notice about yourself and your ministry right now? Where are you going too slowly? In what areas are you going too fast?

» Given what you learn, look at the road ahead. What course corrections or pacing adjustments do you need to make? What feels faithful to God's call for you and your ministry right now?

TAKE IT

» Gather your Launch Team to discuss the step and make concrete plans to take action.

» Depending on the nature of the step, you might need to discuss timing, personnel, and potential impact a little or a lot.

» Go for it!

CELEBRATE IT

» Pull your team back together to celebrate your successes, even if they are only very small "wins."

» As you do, capture stories that represent signs of hope that the vision is moving forward.

LEARN FROM IT

» Debrief what went well and what didn't go so well. What can you learn from this? What would you want to do differently next time?

» Determine who else might be able to give helpful input toward deeper learning, such as your pastor, parents, students, or your volunteer team.

» Based on what you learn, can you see a *next* faithful step?

And finally, bathe all of this process in prayer, step after step after step.

BATHE ALL OF THIS PROCESS IN PRAYER, STEP AFTER STEP AFTER STEP.